THE LIT
BLACK BOOK OF
BUSINESS
SPEAKING

Michael C. Thomsett

amacom

American Management Association

Library of Congress Cataloging-in-Publication Data

Thomsett, Michael C.
    The little black book of business speaking / Michael C. Thomsett.
        p.   cm.
    Includes index.
    ISBN 0-8144-7715-1
    1. Communication in business. 2. Oral communication. 3. Public
speaking. I. Title.
HF5718.T464   1989
658.4'52—dc20   89-45459
                                                                    CIP

Printing number

10 9 8 7 6 5 4 3 2

*2012: Someone said, "It's not the Problems
You have in business that Causes Problems,
its how You deal with them!*

Contents

Introduction

'Tis easier to know how to speak than how to be silent.

—Thomas Fuller

Everyone has something to say—something of value that others need and want to hear. Even when a topic is widely known, your personal observations, trials, and successes add to the general business knowledge important to all of us.

With the communications and automated technology available today, impersonal communication has become not only possible, but practical and efficient. Still, everyone has a driving need to meet with other people face-to-face. In fact, as impersonal technology improves, this need becomes more obvious and more pressing. The demand for what some have called "high touch" is the human element in communication.

A message on paper contains only two dimensions. Businesses are operated by human beings who, in spite of technological advances, are not entirely comfortable without the added third dimension—human contact. There has therefore been no decline in face-to-face meetings, seminars, or conventions, but if anything, an increase.

As your career advances, you will eventually have the opportunity to stand up in front of other people and make a live presentation. Whether it's a small group of executives or several hundred strangers, you will need to master a number of skills in order to carry off your presentation with style and confidence.

No matter how well documented your facts or how well written your material, your audience will respond not to what you say, but to how you say it. We humans shun facts and technology in one respect: We draw conclusions instinctively, based on what we think about the messenger, and those conclusions are often more significant than the message itself. In other words, the demeanor we carry to the podium or to the boardroom is at least as important as the content of the speech.

This book addresses this business reality, especially for the manager who has little or no experience in speaking. If we isolated ourselves and delivered messages to the outside world via memos, letters, computers, and other messengers, we would never have the opportunity to experience this challenge. You will discover that speaking in front of others is a powerful and rewarding form of communication, one that allows you to experience effective interaction directly and immediately.

This *Little Black Book* explores the positive aspects of speaking in a business environment and explains how to overcome the problems that all speakers face: the fear of speaking, the need for preparation, how to deal with nervousness, the speaker's environment, and the audience. It also addresses many of the special situations you will face when you give a speech, shows you how to break down and organize a speech, gives you techniques for presentation, and explains how to use speaking aids. You will find out how to field questions from the audience and how to pick your subject. Each chapter contains a work project to help you develop confidence as a speaker.

Our purpose is not to explain concepts that speakers use to succeed, but to present ideas you can put into use at once. You will become comfortable in facing problems by realizing their solutions. Ultimately, you will be able to accept a speaking assignment confidently and even to seek the opportunity.

With this *Little Black Book,* you will realize that the problems speakers face are simple to overcome—once those problems are defined. Keep this *Little Black Book* locked in your desk or hidden away, so that others cannot discover your secret weapon, or your secret: that speaking is an opportunity not to be missed, and that overcoming fear is a natural result of preparation, organization, and self-confidence.

1

Nervousness: The Self-Defeating Condition

Half the world is composed of people who have something to say and can't, and the other half who have nothing to say and keep on saying it.

—Robert Frost

"Just pretend everyone in the audience is naked," the experienced speaker told the novice. "That will give you a psychological advantage." The young man thought this over a moment and then asked, "Should I forget about having them stand up to ask questions?"

Nearly everyone who gets up in front of others to speak will experience nervousness. This is a natural state, and you can learn to use it as a positive force.

Experienced speakers feel nervous, often to a greater degree than the novice. They understand the condition, and they know that it's not a handicap; rather, it's a prerequisite to becoming the center of attention and being expected to deliver a message. And when a speaker is not nervous immediately before giving a speech, that could mean he or she is *not* well prepared.

Nervousness is nothing more than energy. If not taken under control, it can inhibit you, controlling you physically and preventing you from becoming an effective speaker. But once understood, it is your best weapon and can be used to your advantage.

3

CAUSES OF NERVES

The nervous condition can be described as a circle of fear. Most beginning speakers do not identify their nervous condition as a fear of the audience, or even as the fear of failing as a speaker. In most cases they are nervous about appearing to be nervous.

You may be anxious that your voice will crack or your hands will shake, or that you'll shift from one foot to another. If you've ever been in the audience when an obviously nervous speaker was at the podium, you know how painful that is to watch. And you're afraid the same thing will happen to you. This fear, by itself, can cause the condition to occur.

The solution is to welcome the feeling of nervousness and to learn how to use it to your advantage.

Where does this insecure feeling come from? Of course, you probably already know that on a purely emotional level, no one really wants to stand up before an audience and be exposed to a negative experience. There are four negatives we all fear (see Figure 1-1):

1. *Criticism.* Members of the audience, your supervisor, or your peers might inform you that your speech was not well delivered or well received. They might even offer specific examples of how you *failed* in your delivery. Constructive criticism can be extremely helpful, if you're secure enough and ready to hear it. Mere survival as a speaker is of more immediate concern to the novice; and the novice may be particularly

Figure 1-1.   Negative audience reactions.

criticism
dislike
hostility
apathy

sensitive to criticism, even when it's offered with the best of intentions. If you plan to succeed as a speaker, be prepared to accept honest criticism and to learn from it.

2. *Dislike.* Every speaker's fear can be simplified as the desire to be accepted, coupled with anxiety. What if people do not like you? A speaker must rely on expertise and self-confidence, recognizing that the fear of not being liked is a human condition that invades every aspect of our lives—not just when we speak. For those who stand up in public, when anxiety certainly comes to the surface and becomes obvious, the solution is to *know* that you are qualified to speak on your subject.

3. *Hostility.* As a speaker, you might fear active hostility from your audience. You picture people rising up against you, chasing you from the hall, or interrupting your talk with loud disagreement. As frightening a picture as that presents, it's also very unlikely. For the most part, a passive audience will not collectively lynch a speaker, and a crowd response is very unlikely. It's more probable that individual members will want to confront you on a controversial topic. But if you are presenting information that does not stir people's blood, hostility is the least likely response you will experience.

4. *Apathy.* Most speakers do not even consider apathy as a likely response to their speech. And yet it's more common than hostility. And when you think about it, apathy is more damaging to your self-esteem than an active and verbal assault—because you do not have the opportunity to respond to it. Apathy leaves you with an empty sense of failure that cannot be dealt with or identified specifically. Your response cannot address the issue, because it has never been stated. The uncertainty this creates tends to build over time and to gnaw at the fabric of your self-esteem.

CONFRONTING THE PROBLEM

In order to resolve the insecure feeling that nervousness creates, you must first know how to deal with the four common fears. You could be criticized, disliked, or hated; or your audience might just patiently wait for you to finish and go away. In each of these instances, knowing how *you* can deal with negative responses—should they occur—does help you to overcome that initial feeling of being out of control.

1. *Criticism.* Do not fear your critics. Instead, welcome them as your allies. Recognize criticism as a process that helps you to improve. For example, if someone tells you that one aspect of your speech was flawed, you will know how to correct the problem during your next speech. The only way you can improve is through knowledge. And as a speaker, you might not be aware of a problem until you receive criticism.

Many people who ask for criticism are actually seeking praise. The two are not the same at all. A helpful criticism is one that shows you how to improve in the future. Listen carefully to honest criticism, and learn from it.

2. *Dislike.* You might conclude that your audience did not like you, based on the look on someone's face in the first row; the overall response—or lack of response—from the audience; or something that's said to you.

Regardless of where you get the impression that "they" didn't like you, don't be overly preoccupied about it. In most cases dislike is an individual response rather than a group one. As a comment it's vague and of little value to you. For example, one company presented a series of education symposia and surveyed the audience. Under the "comments" section, one audience member wrote in that he "did not like" one of the speakers. But with no reasons stated, the comment was of absolutely no value. A criticism is specific. Dislike is emotional.

Unless you're given specific reasons why you were disliked as a speaker, ignore this response. Welcome criticism, but only when it is specific and constructive.

3. *Hostility.* Most instances of hostility come up because a speaker failed to understand the audience. Perhaps the message challenges or questions the validity of the group or ridicules an idea they hold sacred.

Before constructing your speech, you must evaluate it in terms of your audience. If your message will create hostility, but you believe you must deliver it that way, you have nothing to be nervous about. You know what reaction to expect, and you will not be surprised when it occurs. Creating hostility can be a very efficient way to bring disagreement into the open—very quickly and without any doubt.

Nervousness about hostility relates more to the unexpected variety. What will you do if the audience reacts strongly to your speech? How will you survive? The answer must go back to your own honesty in putting your message together. If you believe in your own point of view, then you must feel completely justified in holding it—even if you must become a martyr in order to convey that message to others.

You will survive even the unexpected form of hostility. Remember that memory is short-lived, and your audience will probably forget their hostility very quickly. If you deliver a speech at ten in the morning and receive a hostile reaction, the audience will probably forget all about it by the end of the day. So you will survive the experience.

4. *Apathy.* This is by far the most difficult audience response to deal with, because it is not a confrontational situation. A dearth of reaction leaves you with nothing. The apathetic audience doesn't care enough to offer criticism, and is too uninterested to give you even the courtesy of hostility.

The hard truth about apathy is this: It's probably the speaker's own fault. An audience becomes apathetic because the speaker either fails to inspire or delivers a speech that offers nothing new. Apathy is the ultimate expression of boredom.

If you meet with apathy, it's time to admit that you need to go back to the beginning and review the content of your speech, the way you deliver your message, and the way you comprehend the audience.

CHANNELING YOUR NERVOUSNESS

The worst aspect of being nervous is that you don't know what to do to correct it. Most novice speakers just want it to go away so that they won't have to experience it. The anxiety and out-of-control sense a speaker has just before going on is a most troubling sensation—until that speaker learns how to channel nervousness into another form of energy.

The secret about nervousness is this: It *is* a positive form of energy. You feel a knot in your stomach, you perspire, and your hands shake mainly because you don't know what to do to release the energy. Experienced and successful speakers have learned how to harness their nerves to help themselves communicate directly with the audience.

Example: The organizer of a national convention was worried after meeting the keynote speaker an hour before his scheduled speech. The speaker had the reputation of being an inspiring, energetic person who invariably whipped the audience into a receptive mood. But the speaker seemed bland, lacking in energy, and uninteresting. However, when he got up to speak, he was full of energy, his voice rang out, and his gestures seemed to reach directly into the audience. Everyone was caught up in his enthusiasm and energy, and the keynote speech was exactly what it was supposed to be—a big kickoff for a long day of presentations.

What was the speaker's secret? It mattered not that as an individual he was a shy, introverted person who seemed meek and uninteresting. When he stood up to speak, he knew how to channel his nervous energy into a dynamic, powerful expression of ideas.

Some people have a natural gift for speaking and know how to achieve that effect naturally. But for most of us, it takes quite a lot of work. First, you must assume that the message you have to deliver is well organized and interesting enough to excite members of an audience—or at least to hold their attention. That in itself is a big order. But as long as you have sincere enthusiasm and passion for your topic, you certainly can create an enthusiastic and passionate audience as well—by learning to use nervousness to your advantage.

The problem most beginners face is that they don't know how to use energy as a positive force. The beginner is more immediately concerned with getting through the speech. The speaker who does not understand the causes of nervousness tries to make it go away. And logically, we all know that's impossible. You will discover that survival becomes an assumed fact after a few modest successes. With very little experience, you will find yourself thinking more in terms of the intensity with which you deliver your message, and not just worrying about surviving your time at the podium.

The first step must be getting your nervousness under control. You cannot allow yourself to get up and speak when you're not in control of your body. Most speakers discover that the nervousness is most intense just before they stand up. As soon as they begin to speak, it is reduced significantly and may even go away completely.

This is a dangerous point in your speech. If you become too relaxed, you will be relieved, thinking you have conquered the greatest threat. In fact, your task has just begun. If you're too relaxed, your energy level falls, you will not be as intense as you should, and you might even put your audience to sleep.

You'll do much better if you hold onto your nervousness and learn to control it. Here are a few ideas to achieve this (see Figure 1-2):

1. *Use the actor's technique for developing the power of concentration.* Focus your attention on an object until you feel more relaxed. Then adjust your focus to a smaller object and finally to a very specific object. These "circles of concentration" are used in the theater to stay in character while on stage and also to prepare for an entrance. They relax you. They do not make nervousness go away, but do shift your attention away from the sensation of being out of control and emphasize the message you'll deliver.

2. *Stop fighting your nerves.* The harder you swallow, the more you tense up, and the more pacing you do, the more you accelerate your

Figure 1-2. Checklist: controlling nervousness.

1. Concentrate on an object.

2. Stop fighting your nerves.

3. Tense and relax your muscles.

4. Stretch your muscles.

5. Speak with someone else.

6. Go through your self-esteem checklist.

7. Increase your energy level.

nervousness. Relax, take several deep breaths, and pay attention to what's going on. You will quickly discover that the tight stomach and sweating palms are not out of your control.

3. *Tense and relax your muscles.* Try this with your hands, feet, and neck—the three places where you're most likely to feel the physical effects of nerves.

4. *Stretch your arms, legs, and neck after the tense and relax exercise.*

5. *Speak with someone else before you go on, preferably about something other than your speech.* Don't put your energy into discussing what you're going to say, and don't talk about being nervous. Relax by creating a brief interaction with someone, even if only for a moment of small talk.

6. *Go through a personal self-esteem checklist.* You are an expert, you communicate well, you have an important message to deliver, and you are enthusiastic about your own point of view. Decide that you're going to have a good time giving your speech.

7. *Consciously increase the level of energy you are feeling.* Nervousness is nothing more than energy. But rather than trying to make it go away, accelerate it. With the exercises you're practicing, you now have your nerves under control and channeled. It's time now to prepare yourself to get up and deliver a speech full of energy, so that your enthusiasm will be conveyed to the audience.

MEETING YOUR AUDIENCE

Some speakers make the mistake of isolating themselves before they deliver their speech. Like the actor, who is not supposed to have any contact with the audience before making the big entrance, speakers think they're obligated to suffer bravely through their nervousness on their own.

This misconception only inhibits the sincere communication that every speaker wants to achieve. It not only helps to have direct contact with members of your audience before you speak; it might make the difference between an acceptable but bland talk and an exciting, inspiring presentation.

The reason? If you have developed personal contact by the time you stand up at the podium, you can direct your speech at the one person you met a few minutes beforehand. This is one technique for conquering nervousness, and it works because we prefer singular contacts. It's much easier to speak with one other person than to deal with the little-understood crowd personality. Most beginning speakers fail to realize that people in a large group are extremely passive and will allow you far more lattitude than one other person will. They're more likely to accept your ideas, less likely to challenge you, and certainly not as likely to interrupt you as you speak.

Still, if you try the techniques for controlling and channeling your energy, and they simply don't work as well as you'd like, go out of your way to meet one or more of the members of your audience before you stand up in front of them.

One speaker was exceptionally nervous and knew she would have to get it under control before getting up to speak. Fortunately, just before her speech, there was a 15-minute coffee break. Her first impulse was to stay away from the foyer where the audience gathered and remain in the meeting room by herself. But instead she went out and introduced herself to several people.

When she was introduced at the podium, she quickly located one of the people she'd spoken to during the break. Her entire speech was directed to that person. It helped her to control her nerves, relax enough to concentrate on her speaking style, and channel her energy the way she wanted. It proved to be a very effective technique.

Another speaker discovered the same technique when he delivered his first speech, but in a different way. His supervisor attended the meeting with him and saw that the young man was very nervous. He made a suggestion: "I'm going to sit in the last row. Look for me, and deliver the entire speech directly at me. Pretend there's no one else in the room."

The speaker used that technique and it worked well. The next time he gave a speech, he asked a friend to serve the same purpose—his audience ally. After delivering many speeches, the speaker was able to use a similar technique—pretending someone in the back row was the sole listener, even without having spoken to him or her ahead of time.

Even experienced speakers can be taken by surprise and may find themselves unexpectedly uneasy about a particular speech. One consultant arrived at a convention site to deliver two speeches in the same day. He discovered that the meeting room was relatively small and set up in a workshop format. That meant more interaction. The audience would be closer than it is in the setting of more traditional, staged talks.

To deal with his nervous energy, the speaker waited outside the room and, as audience members arrived, he greeted them. It required only a nod and a smile or a brief word in most cases. But the direct contact immediately before giving the speech did a great deal to reassure the speaker. When he went in and began his talk, he simply located someone near the back of the room whom he had greeted, and he made that person his audience ally.

ACKNOWLEDGING YOUR NERVOUSNESS

Don't be a brave martyr as you prepare yourself for your speech. If someone asks you whether you're nervous, say yes and don't elaborate any farther. Dwelling on the condition is contrary to your purpose, which is to channel that sense of fear into a positive and useful speaker's tool.

Denying nervousness is the same thing as denying energy. If you accept the idea that nervousness is a natural condition, then there is no point in denying it. Some speakers confuse fear with cowardice, believing that an admission of nervousness proves they're not brave. If you are truly nervous, it's probably obvious to people, and they may ask if you're nervous only as a way of expressing sympathy or understanding. A denial does nothing for you; it only makes the condition worse, because it adds an element of shame to the equation.

The experience of fear does not make a speaker a coward. Fear is a natural process in the speaking experience. A coward is one who goes through an entire lifetime able to avoid public speaking through lies and excuses. You may find it necessary to your career to face your fears, no matter how intensely you experience them, and learn to master the speaker's art.

Admitting nervousness to an audience is one very effective technique for overcoming it, as many speakers have discovered by mistake. It's ironic that acknowledging the sensation often places it under control, immediately.

Example: • A speaker practices all of the techniques of concentration, tensing and relaxing, stretching, and so forth, to get his nerves under control. But when he steps up to the podium, his self-confidence is gone and the feeling of nervousness is stronger than ever. So he opens his speech by saying, "I am more nervous about speaking before this group than I've ever been before."

In most cases this simple declaration achieves two significant results. First, members of the audience become very sympathetic. Admitting your nervousness to them creates an immediate bond of understanding. The second result is that the sense of out-of-control nervousness disappears—perhaps in response to the immediate sympathy of the audience.

This simple technique has worked for many speakers, but only when delivered with sincerity. It's a mistake to believe that you can simply plan to start every speech with an admission of nerves and not prepare yourself in any other way. Reserve this move only for those times when, no matter how well you plan and prepare yourself, you simply cannot conquer the condition.

Some speakers have discovered—to their own surprise—that they do better than they thought they could when under pressure. One speaker was so nervous that he couldn't even begin his speech. To buy time, he impulsively decided to tell a joke. It was so well received that he told another, and then another. After a few minutes of making friends with his audience, he was relaxed, felt accepted, and was ready to begin the speech he'd planned. The only difficulty he had at that point was forcing himself to stop the jokes and get down to business.

Starting a speech on a light note is a very effective way to make an immediate breakthrough with your audience. This assumes, of course, that a joke is well received. If it backfires, it makes the experience very hard to survive, because instead of immediate acceptance, you now have immediate rejection. So speakers often do not try to begin with humor. The risk of failure is too high.

One speaker began each talk with a brief comment in a humorous vein. However, he never planned it. The "right thing to say" always seemed to occur to him once he found himself at the podium. Realizing that this was a lucky gift, he never tried to write his opening beforehand. He simply trusted his fate to spontaneity, and it never failed him.

One example of how this worked: The speaker was asked to talk about contracts before an audience of salespeople. He was introduced by Ted, the president of the company. Ted set up the speech by commenting, "Our next speaker will explain the importance of the contract you get the customer to sign." When the speaker took the podium, he borrowed an expression from Samuel Goldwyn and personalized it by saying, "Ted's right; written contracts are important. However, he and I have only a verbal contract, which isn't worth the paper it's written on."

AVOIDING FAILURE

Expressed in a negative way, success could be defined as the avoidance of failure. For speakers who are concerned with surviving the experience of standing up in front of other people, failure becomes a very tangible and threatening possibility, and it's easy for a nervous speaker to begin thinking in very negative terms.

The process of conquering and controlling fear—as it expresses itself through the energy of your nervousness—is different for everyone. Some people prefer to deal with it privately, others simply refuse to acknowledge it, and some of us have to put ourselves through an elaborate process of self-preparation. You might need the crutch of prepared humor, preparatory techniques for building energy or self-esteem, or a specific audience ally. But whatever techniques work for you, the best way to put yourself in control is to make speaking an enjoyable experience.

Being the center of attention, and having the chance to express your own ideas, is an opportunity. Most of us are not celebrities, so we do not have a ready press through which to air our views publicly. Only as speakers can we express ourselves so freely.

Being a speaker does not have to be an experience in fear that drains all of your energy. It can be an exciting and fulfilling experience, if you allow yourself to succeed and to enjoy it. After one or two successes, you will find yourself looking for the chance to speak publicly. You will welcome nervousness once you recognize what it is and discover how to control it.

WORK PROJECT

1. Name two of the four negative reactions you might receive from your audience. Explain how to deal with each.

2. Describe three techniques or exercises for controlling nervousness, and how they help you.

3. What are two techniques for relating with your audience that help deal with nervousness?

2

The Speaker's Secret: Thorough Preparation

He knew the precise psychological moment when to say nothing.

—Oscar Wilde

A speaker arrived moments before his scheduled start time, without notes. He quickly scribbled an outline of his speech on a piece of paper and approached the podium. As he began, the speaker looked at his notes, paused, and then announced, "I'm sorry, I'll have to do this from memory. I can't read my handwriting."

A speaker who lacks self-confidence or enthusiasm for the subject does not improve by working on the content of the speech itself. The real work in preparation for a speech must take place on two levels. First, work on your personal confidence and self-esteem. Second, outline your speech. Your outline must be logical, concise, and appropriate for the subject as well as for the audience.

The longer the time you have until the day of your speech, the greater the opportunity to prepare—in one sense. You do have time for research, revisions to the outline, and planning. But time can also work against you. If doubts and nervousness about the speech worsen during your preparation stage, put the outline aside for a few days. Go back to it only after reflecting on the purpose of your speech: what you want to convey, the primary message, and the narrowest possible focus for your speech.

BUILDING YOUR OUTLINE

A very preliminary outline serves to focus a speech narrowly and identify subject matter of interest to the audience. It helps you avoid wasting time on information you do not need to include in your presentation.

To construct an outline that will work, start with a very general list describing the speech. Then revise, adding meat to the bone, gradually building the final outline and more details you'll use. If you are very familiar with your subject, you have an advantage. You will be confident when the audience asks questions and you will not worry that you have nothing of value to communicate.

You also have a disadvantage. You might be so close to your subject that it will be difficult to distinguish between what's interesting to you and what your audience wants to know. In this instance you must consider the audience and make every attempt to view your subject from someone else's point of view. What's relevant to people in your audience? What information do you have that they need to hear? How can you communicate your message so that it's interesting to them?

Example: The manager of a data processing department was asked to give a speech on the subject of converting from manual to automated processing. The audience was made up of other managers, who would benefit most from hearing about how to avoid pitfalls, how other managers can deal with the difficulties of change, what to expect along the way, and procedures for protecting files during the conversion and testing period. The manager who was to speak, was so closely involved in the day-to-day problems and operations of the new system that he forgot to consider what the audience wanted to know. Instead of addressing a few key points about the conversion process, he spoke about the way his department operated now—after the conversion was complete. Of course, most of the presentation was extremely uninteresting to the people in the audience. Their departments were not yet automated, so they could not benefit from hearing about the problems and solutions faced by a data processing department. They could not identify with the speaker.

If the manager had taken a little time to think about the audience, he would have realized what the speech should focus on. Without that focus, the speech could not succeed. And the two aspects of preparation—the material and the speaker's own confidence and impression—must be unified, or the speech will not work. No matter how well prepared the speaker is mentally, the material must be appropriate for the audience.

In order to ensure that your speech is both focused and directly at your audience, follow these guidelines for organizing your outline (see Figure 2-1):

1. *Identify pivotal information.* Don't organize your first-draft outline like a job description, or as a summary of the things that interest

Figure 2-1.   Organizing the outline.

1. Identify pivotal information.
2. Make extensive notes.
3. Outline the first draft.
4. Write opening and closing statements.
5. Revise your initial outline.
6. Edit the outline.
7. Allow yourself one rehearsal.
8. Add specific language.
9. Write the final outline.
10. Put the outline aside.

you. Instead, take this approach: Write down on paper the most important aspects of your subject, as though you had to explain it to someone who had never heard of it before. Identify the pivotal information your audience needs.

Example: You will be speaking on the subject of publicity, and your audience will be made up of owners of small businesses. They will not need to hear about why they need publicity; they already understand that issue. Of greater concern is the question "How do I get the best publicity for the least amount of expense?" This should serve as the pivot for your speech.

Center your entire outline around the main points you identify. Don't try to make a speech comprehensive when it should be very narrow. Most audiences lose interest very quickly when speakers are too general in the information they present.

2. *Make extensive notes.* Can you think of five to ten points that your audience needs to hear? We must assume that you were asked to give a speech because you know your subject better than anyone else does. Be willing to give your listeners as many points of great value as possible, so that the information they hear from you makes a difference in their method of operation or changes their attitude.

For example, in speaking about ways to get publicity, list five to ten ideas that audience members probably have not considered trying. As an expert in your subject, you are more qualified than anyone else to come up with these points. They will make interesting subject matter in your speech.

3. *Outline the first draft.* If you find it useful, use index cards at this point (even if you don't plan to use cards in your actual speech). Experiment with presenting information in different formats.

While your speech should ultimately be highly conversational, your notes should be organized in outline form. You will not read your outline, but you will structure your speech around the outline format. As you experiment with varying arrangements of information, keep this important point in mind: Look for a format that lends itself to the logical sequence of a conversation.

One technique that helps this process is to pretend that you're giving your speech to a friend at an informal setting. What are the most important things your friend should know about the subject? What should you say first and, when you've said it, what questions does your statement raise?

By following the course of the imaginary conversation, the most comfortable and logical flow of your speech will present itself. You will probably discover that there is one best way to organize your outline and present your speech. By taking the time to discover it, you demonstrate an understanding of your audience.

4. *Write opening and closing statements.* These are the only sections of your speech you actually need to write out and read from your cards. The body of the speech should be delivered from the broad outline. In the opening you can use humor, anecdotes, or attention-getting statistics. You should also define the scope of what you plan to cover in the speech.

Example: To start out a speech about getting publicity, an opening statement can be designed to get the audience's attention. You might start out by saying, "Most small business owners make the mistake of paying for publicity. Why pay for something you can get for free?" Following this, tell the audience what you plan to explain in the body of the speech: "There are five effective ways to reach your markets without spending money on expensive ads." From there you can go directly into the body of the speech.

The conclusion should wrap up and summarize your main message, or it should end with a reassuring, final statement.

Example of main message summary: "With these five techniques, you will be able to trim your advertising budget. At the same time you will increase the valuable market contacts you need."

Example of a reassuring final statement: "These five levels of contact do not require a publicity or public relations expert. They're best executed by the person who knows your business better than anyone else—yourself."

5. *Revise your initial outline.* Revise your notes with the introduction and conclusion in mind. You will discover at this point that some of the subject matter you planned to cover will change, or that yet another rearrangement is in order. In some cases, coming up with the best opening and closing remarks dictates a new and better focus for the entire speech.

Example: Your first outline includes a discussion of different ways to get publicity, including both paid and free outlets. But once your opening and closing statements are finalized, you see that the speech should concentrate on *free* publicity. You remove all discussion of paid ads.

6. *Edit the outline.* Look for parts of the outline that you can reduce or eliminate. Constantly attempt to narrow the focus of your presentation. If you have eight major points to convey, can you cut them down to five or six? The more trimming you do at this point, the better your focus.

Example: You have cut your original outline down to only the free sources for publicity. At this point you have nine possible methods, but four of them are not very strong and will not work for most businesses. You eliminate these and decide to concentrate on your five strongest ideas.

7. *Allow yourself one rehearsal.* Avoid actually talking through the entire presentation. Just go over the outline, thinking about the way you will present what you have to say.

Emphasis should be on the conversation you want to hold with your audience. No one enjoys being spoken to; most people want to believe they are being spoken with. Even when your audience consists of several hundred people, you will be most successful when you make most of the individuals feel as though your speech addresses issues of concern to them.

8. *Add specific language.* Write out brief sections of your speech, but only when you want to make major points. Keeping in mind the point that you only need to write out your opening and closing remarks, you might also find it useful to write out the precise wording for a few key points. This is an effective technique to use during your speech. Break away from the conversational flow to read a statement from your notes. That draws attention to your statement.

Example: During your speech about getting publicity, you follow your outline in a conversational style until you reach your first key point. You then pause and read the statement "When you send news releases to the business editor of your local paper, remember three things. First, most news releases are thinly disguised public relations announcements that end up in the wastebasket. Second, the editor welcomes real news. And third, you must follow up your release with a telephone call."

Using the three-part argument for your key points is one of the best ways to draw attention to your material. People respond well to this technique.

9. *Write the final outline.* After sketching and revising your speech through the steps above, you are now ready to commit your presentation outline to paper. Think ahead to the speech itself, and then decide whether to use paper, a legal pad, index cards, or some other medium for conveniently storing your notes. Make your decision based on the speaking environment. Will you have a podium? Will the speech be delivered while you're standing or will you be sitting at a roundtable? What method of recording notes will you find to be the most comfortable?

10. *Put the outline aside.* Do not review the outline again until the day of your speech. Unless you change your mind about the outline itself, you should not spend time rehearsing or worrying about how you will do. Put the speech out of your mind for now, and think only about the positive mental images that will make it possible for you to convey your message with confidence and self-assurance.

WRITING THE OUTLINE

When you are given a speaking assignment, chances are that it will be overly broad. That means it's up to you to narrow your focus. You can't expect a seminar organizer, your supervisor, or the president of the company to plan your speech for you, nor to provide you with the right focus for the audience.

As the expert in your subject, you must take a broad assignment and make it interesting for your audience—by focusing the subject matter down to a short list of big points.

Example: An accounting manager is assigned the task of presenting a speech to a seminar attended by managers, on the subject of budgeting. That is extremely broad, since there are many aspects and points of view on that topic. He chooses the title "Budgets: Your Hidden Profit Center." His purpose is to present budgeting from the point of view that, correctly used, it can actually serve as a management technique for control. As a result, profits can be estimated and created.

Even with that emphasis, the topic is still a broad one. The accountant has to narrow the focus by picking a few important aspects concerning the process and concentrating on them. He might assume that the people in the audience already understand the budgeting process, that they do not need a lecture about their responsibilities for projecting future expenses, and that most of them are frustrated by the budgeting process as it's usually done.

These assumptions lead to some conclusions that help narrow the focus of the speech. The accountant decides to focus on discussing ways to make budgets tangible and necessary processes for effective management. His audience, he concludes, needs insights about how to make the process less mysterious, more useful, and more relevant to each manager's objectives.

He develops an outline in which the opening and closing statements are written out, with the major points in between broken out into major sections. (see Figure 2-2 for a summary of these sections.)

The budget speech outline:

Opening comment
Accountants are famous for their analysis of budget variances. This is *not* an exciting or positive image. In fact, as an accountant myself, I've been compared to the soldier. My job is to go out onto the battlefield after the battle has been fought and bayonet the wounded.

Focus comments
- Budgets are useless, unless used to generate profits.
- Budgets are also useless without a means for reacting to what the process reveals.
- Budgets are highly political tools in your corporate culture.

Problems
- You know how to budget already.
- You are not allowed to budget logically.

- You have difficulty influencing change in your corporate culture when it comes to budgeting.

Solutions
- You can train top management by showing them better ways to budget.
- The technique of profit-center budgeting is easily explained and easily proven.
- Influencing change in your culture requires the use of a few communication techniques.

Closing comment
Top management may be stubborn in their resistance to change. But they will always welcome new ideas that are tied to the one thing they're sure to understand: profits. And every one of you can make a difference once you realize that budgets should be, and can be, one of your most powerful management tools.

In this outline the accountant is faced with a formidable task: explaining budgeting in such a way that the audience's interest is kept alive. He plans to open with a humorous comment. This not only breaks the initial tension of getting up to speak; it also lets the audience know— at once—that the speaker, an accountant himself, sees the humor in the stereotypical image of his profession. This gets the audience on his side.

From there he immediately jumps into his focus comments, a series of revealing promises. Rather than merely discussing the mundane subject of budgeting, the real focus of this speech concerns an issue that every manager deals with each day: the sense of futility in dealing with top management. Budgets, the speech's focus contends, are one way to make a difference. The futility managers feel toward the budgeting process can be turned around. This is a big promise, but the accountant knows he can deliver on it.

After introducing his focus comments, the accountant raises several problems. This adds an element of insight that the audience members may never be able to express clearly. It also directs the audience toward the focus of the more detailed section of the speech that follows.

The solutions section is the part of the speech that will take the most time, because many details will be discussed and explained. Throughout,

Figure 2-2.   Outline sequence.

```
┌─────────────┐
│  opening    │
│  comment    │
└─────────────┘
       │
┌─────────────┐
│  focus      │
│  comments   │
└─────────────┘
       │
┌─────────────┐
│  problems   │
│             │
└─────────────┘
       │
┌─────────────┐
│  solutions  │
│             │
└─────────────┘
       │
┌─────────────┐
│  closing    │
│  comment    │
└─────────────┘
```

the accountant knows he will have to express ideas in terms of immediate interest to the managers, and not just from the point of view of the accounting department.

The concluding comment wraps up the main point. Again, the speech is not about budgets, but how to use the budgeting process to improve the degree of positive influence each manager can exercise in his or her company.

With a well-developed outline, the speaker gives his listeners information of direct value. The accountant's experience and insights can help them to participate in the budgeting process so that they can control, direct, and increase profits. Management can be taught to appreciate a more logical and intelligent approach. That's the real message, and the real focus.

Such a speech will be inspiring to the audience, because it is both valuable and sympathetic. This dual benefit is achieved with a rather brief outline, which keeps the speaker on the subject and directs the audience toward a very narrow theme.

The alternative is to prepare a rather uninteresting and redundant discourse on budgeting in general. It could be very broad and comprehensive, covering the process and procedure as perceived in the corporate world. It could fill up the entire time allotted, without providing anything that members of the audience can use. And if it's prepared like a good number of speeches, it could be presented from the speaker's point of view, and not the audience's. In this instance one thing is certain: It will not be an interesting speech.

When a poorly directed or poorly focused speech is over, the speaker must conclude that in spite of his or her extensive preparation the audience was not receptive. The most common conclusion in this case is to say, "Next time I'll spend more time on the outline." The mistake, of course, is that this approach doesn't consider the real problem: The speech was *not* interesting to the audience. This is the essential element to remember in the outline. Any speaker who devotes time and energy only to develop subject matter will never feel comfortable behind a podium. But by focusing material, and by thinking of the subject from the audience's point of view, a speaker will succeed—even when the subject is as dry and unexciting as the budgeting process.

THE UNEXPECTED SPEECH

You might not have time to prepare an outline for your speech at all. In fact, many speakers will tell you that the best speeches they've ever given were thrust upon them unexpectedly.

Example: A manager attended a seminar his company sponsored. During an evening banquet the president made a few announcements and then called the manager to the podium. Completely unprepared, the manager went up, assuming the president wanted him to introduce the next speaker. He quietly asked the president, "What do you want me to say?" The president answered, "You have 15 minutes. Tell a few jokes."

The manager turned around and looked at the audience and then spent 15 minutes performing. He had no prepared material, and he had no idea what he was going to say. But when his time was up, the president had to step in to get him to stop. The manager later admitted, "If I'd had time to prepare, I never would have been able to get through it."

Some people have the gift of responding well to the unexpected and can be spontaneous under pressure. Others do not have this gift. You have no way of knowing how you will perform in a spontaneous situation—until *your* president sets you up in the same way.

Whether you're suddenly called upon to amuse, inform, or inspire an audience, you will have one big advantage. Without the time to prepare, you will not be able to develop the nervousness that speakers invariably go through as they think ahead to their speech. If this happens to you, always depend on your expertise to carry you through. Deal with issues you know well.

In the example above, the president knew that the manager he called on had an arsenal of good stories to tell. The manager depended on his timing and sense of humor and did well in an unexpected situation.

Few people will welcome being called on to deliver a speech without any preparation. One consultant had that experience when he attended a training seminar one of his clients put on for marketing representatives. When he arrived at the meeting at 9:45, he picked up a program and discovered that he was scheduled to deliver a 45-minute talk, starting at 10 o'clock. No one had bothered to tell him that he was on the program. The only fact that saved him was his expertise. He knew the subject well because he was a specialist, and he was able to deliver an informative talk.

RESEARCHING YOUR FACTS

The first-time speaker must confront the problem not only of what to talk about, but also of what information to include in a speech. A first assumption is that a worthwhile speech must be filled with quotations and statistics. But in many cases the audience will appreciate a more personal approach, including

- Your own observations or ideas
- Your experiences
- Your direct knowledge

We all have ideas that have developed from observation. A speech is enjoyable on its own when these ideas are well expressed and shared—merely as observations. It takes much more energy to prepare a speech that involves a large number of statistics designed to support your ideas. Such a speech is also less enjoyable to listen to.

Experiences shared during a speech can be the most informative *and* entertaining parts. This is especially so if you have amusing, salient stories that illustrate an important point. Experience expressed through humor is remembered by the audience and is also informative.

Your own knowledge is probably the reason you are asked to give a speech. It's an honor to receive that form of acknowledgment from a supervisor or executive, even though it seems more like a threatening imposition on your self-esteem and sense of anonymous security.

The combination of observations, experience, and knowledge may be all you need to deliver an excellent speech. If you try to go beyond these, you risk losing the human touch by adding more than you actually need. However, there are speeches that do require research.

Before assuming that the historical record, the library, or periodicals are your best sources for information, consider the research outlets close at hand and use them as sources for information:

1. *Other managers.* You will discover that other people in your company can supply you with information to add depth to your speech. Of even greater value, the manager in a different department can add a point of view to your subject that you might not have considered.

Example: A marketing manager is preparing a speech she will give before an audience of accountants. The subject is "How to Prepare Income Forecasts." During the preparatory stages the manager lists the best ways to document assumptions about future revenues, broken down by sales division, recruiting assumptions, and trends based on years of experience. Before finalizing the outline, she meets with her company's accountant to discuss the speech. The accountant points out that the audience—other accountants—will be less concerned with the methods of building forecasts than with the ways to track variances, identify problems, and develop methods to reverse negative trends.

As a result of these insights, the marketing manager revises her speech with the audience in mind.

2. *Employees in your department.* The people working for you or with you could prove to be your best sources for information, especially when your speech will be on a topic they know. A manager may be given the actual speaking assignment when one or more employees are actually closer to the issues.

Example: The manager of a customer relations department was asked to give a speech about tracking customer contact and response. It was a large department, and the manager spent most of her time dealing with personnel issues and budgets. Her assistant was more directly involved in the day-to-day system. The manager met with her assistant and was able to expand the scope of the speech beyond its original concept.

3. *Executives.* Top management in your company can be used as resources for your speech. Their point of view will invariably differ from yours, and you will discover that the "larger picture" is of great value to you.

Example: A manager was given the assignment to deliver a speech at a convention of corporate executives, on the subject of project scheduling and control. The manager discussed the speech with his company's president and discovered that the techniques being used in his department had many applications for executives. In fact, the president used many techniques that were similar to the manager's. But the manager's perspective was directed toward details, reports, and short-term budgets. The president emphasized market factors: the competition, market share, long-term planning, and profitability. This helped the manager develop an outline with a point of view more directed to the audience.

PLANNING FOR CONFRONTATION

The information you present in your speech might go against traditional thinking and even upset members of your audience. There is nothing wrong with debate nor with controversy. However, people resist change, and when ideas go against their beliefs they might react with hostility. As a speaker, how can you prepare for this possibility?

Example: A consultant spoke before an audience of stockbrokers, concerning the commission compensation system. His main point was that when stockbrokers are paid by commission they cannot avoid a conflict of interest. He knew that many members of the audience would not like hearing his message.

In the preparation phase, the consultant made several notes about points he wanted to cover, including

- The stockbroker has as much of a dilemma as the customer.
- Doing away with commissions altogether would also remove the incentive to succeed.
- Alternatives must be devised that will solve the problems of customers *and* stockbrokers.

This initial three-point message will not completely do away with controversy. However, it does set the ground for intelligent dialogue rather than polarized opinions. From this premise the speech was developed not to point out flaws, but to propose specific solutions.

The confrontation you are most likely to encounter will come not from individual members of your audience, but from the audience as a whole. Anticipating that event, you must be prepared to make your speech both honest and sympathetic. If you audience has a strong point of view about your topic—stockbrokers and commission payments, for example—you should not plan to attack the system directly. Instead, structure your speech to identify sympathetically with *the audience's* problem. Then offer constructive ideas to solve that problem.

You will not always have enough time to think about how to deal with hostility from your audience. It could take you by surprise. But as long as you have a sincere, honest message to deliver, containing information your audience needs to hear, your speech will succeed.

Example: An attorney was scheduled to speak at 1 P.M. The previous speaker wrapped up his speech concerning trends in litigation, ending with the remark that there were too many lawyers in the country, and they all ought to be tarred and feathered and run out of town on a rail. The audience gave a standing ovation. Then it was the lawyer's turn.

Taken completely off guard, he realized that the opening he intended to use would no longer work. So he stepped up to the podium, looked out at the audience quietly for several moments, and then remarked, "I just want to warn you: If I see a bucket of tar, I'm out of here."

When the lawyer first stepped up to the podium, hostility was in the air. Taking a long pause and then delivering the opening line, he turned the mood completely around. He turned a hostile mob into a roomful of friends and allies, simply by making a humorous, timely remark. Without that opening his 60-minute speech could have been the longest hour of his life.

Audiences are pliable. They do not hold absolute opinions and can be swayed from one extreme to the other, often with a simple, well-timed statement. You must be prepared to deal with confrontations, especially the unexpected ones. Always keep in mind that your purpose is to deliver a well-focused message and to deliver it well. If you decide that the message is not getting through, or that the people in your audience will not be receptive to what you plan to say, you must be able to turn them around—or to face the confrontation and deal with it directly.

WORK PROJECT

1. What parts of your speech should be written out and read, and how does that device help you dramatize and draw attention to your primary message?

2. Name the three best sources for developing your speech, from outlets close at hand.

3. List two research sources and describe how they can help you expand the point of view of your speech.

3

The Big Fear: Standing Up and Speaking Out

Remember that every time you open your mouth to talk, your mind walks out and parades up and down the words.

—Edwin H. Stuart

A manager gave his first speech to an audience of over 300 insurance agents. When a friend asked him how it went, the manager answered, "Not well. After it was over, no one even tried to sell me a policy."

We all desire success and want to have a sense of accomplishment in every aspect of our lives. And success does breed more success. But no matter how much self-confidence you have, and no matter how many times you have succeeded in the past, being asked to get up in front of others and speak for the first time can shake your confidence and bring up many doubts and fears.

A successful first speech is reassuring and may lead to a repeat of the experience. But the fear of speaking will not necessarily go away after the first time. It could get worse. And if your first time out as a speaker is not a big success, you'll have more problems preparing for your second speech.

People fear having to speak in front of a group, perhaps more than any other act they will be required to perform. Yet the speaking experience is an opportunity to project a positive, high profile—one that will add to your influence in the company, as well as to your self-esteem. As a career businessperson, you will eventually have the opportunity to stand up and demonstrate your positive talents and knowledge. But without knowing how to prepare yourself for this test, you will indeed be a victim to nerves. Fear of speaking could control you, rather than the other way around.

DEALING WITH FEAR

There are solutions to this problem, and they're not as difficult as most first-time speakers believe. In order to conquer fear, we must first understand its origins. Fear comes from not knowing what to expect. The solution is to script not only your speech, but the impression you make while delivering that speech. For the inexperienced speaker, knowing how to overcome the fear is itself a challenge—because the problem itself is not fully understood.

Speaking is nothing more than an efficient form of communication. It's efficient because feedback is instantaneous. You see it in the audience mood; on the facial expressions of those before you; and in the applause, laughter, or intense silence of full concentration. A memo or report conveys facts and can be organized to supply a lot of details. A speaker, though, interacts with an audience, adding a human element to the communication of facts.

To overcome your initial fear of speaking, keep these points in mind and then ask yourself three questions:

1. *Concentrate on the subject as an initial step in preparation.* Most people who are asked to speak are assumed to have a degree of expertise in their subject. So take the approach that you are, indeed an expert. Your first question should be, *"What do I know about the subject that other people want to hear?"*

2. *Think about the people in your audience.* What do they already know and how can you add to their knowledge? Your speech should

both confirm and enlighten. To make your speech valuable, ask the question, *"What does the audience already know about my subject?"*

3. *Once you understand your own level of knowledge and what the audience already knows, you need only to identify what remains in the equation.* Your third question is, *"What does the audience need to hear about my subject?"* The relationship of the three questions is shown in Figure 3-1.,

You certainly do not want to waste your listeners' time by telling them things they already know. However, you might do well by including an appropriate amount of information that confirms their beliefs or knowledge.

Example: You have been asked to give a speech to an audience of managers, on the subject of supervising the difficult employee. As a manager yourself, you recognize the problems your audience faces each day. You decide to include a sympathetic message at the beginning of your speech, identifying the problem of supervision.

By starting off a speech in this manner, you will immediately gain your listeners' attention. Even though you start out with something they already know, you make it clear that you're talking directly to them.

Figure 3-1.   Defining the subject.

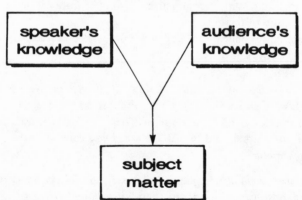

You are addressing the frustrations they face, and that will create allies in your audience.

Starting out with sympathetic comments is one of the best ways to quickly get the audience on your side. If you can devise a way to do this in your speech, you will conquer a large part of your fear.

THE ORIGIN OF FEAR

We are afraid to speak because we do not know what to expect. In addition, we do not want to find ourselves in the spotlight with no control. And, of course, we fear failing in that situation.

All of these attributes may be expressed as a general fear of public speaking. But each one is easily overcome. This is not to say that a sense of nervousness will disappear simply by understanding why speaking is such an intimidating experience. But you can learn to make nervousness a tool rather than a handicap. It is nothing more than energy, and it can be directed and channeled to add power to your speaking experience.

Not knowing what to expect is a natural fear for anyone who has never given a speech. It also relates to not knowing how your listeners will respond to you. The unspoken part of this fear is "What if they don't like me?" And that is best dealt with by doing away with your assumptions about audiences.

A key point to keep in mind is this: While there may be hostile individuals out there, the people in your audience, for the most part, want you to give a good speech. They want you to succeed. One of the most uncomfortable experiences is sitting in an audience while a speaker struggles with nerves. The voice cracks, the feet shift, the speaker loses notes, repeats, or simply freezes up and must be taken off. No one wants to see that happen to you or to anyone else.

To deal with the fear of the unknown as a speaker, abandon any assumptions you're making about your audience. You're unlikely to meet with hostility, interruptions, or apathy as long as you bring energy, confidence, enthusiasm, and information with you.

Assumptions include the following self-defeating statements you may find yourself making:

1. No one wants to hear anything I would have to say to them.
2. I have a boring job and a flat image. What could the audience possibly find interesting about me?
3. Someone else could do a better job.

You must abandon these assumptions at the very beginning of your speaking experience—in the preparation stages. Otherwise, you will never be able to overcome the fear of speaking, and you'll never be able to give a good speech.

Anyone can succeed as a speaker, but few people have learned the techniques of effective speaking. Those who have do not possess any complicated secrets, they are not necessarily charismatic individuals, and they have no more self-confidence than you do. They've simply learned to channel their attitudes and perceptions, both about themselves and about their audiences.

This fact is not just a positive thinking concept, although positive thinking is certainly a big part of it, but a realistic preparatory stage that every successful speaker must go through. Just as the athlete must warm up physically before a big race, the speaker must warm up mentally, apply the correct attitude, and use the right self-esteem techniques to prepare for a successful talk.

Example: A data processing manager was asked to speak about the controls needed in an automated system, and he was allotted two hours. His first reaction was to think, "This is going to bore the audience to tears."

If the speaker accepts that premise, then certainly the speech will be a huge failure. The alternative is to take advantage of the opportunity to dispel the myth about controls as a boring subject, and take the approach that the audience needs and wants to learn certain facts about how to do their job more effectively. The manager may decide to start out the speech by directly confronting the myth that controls are nothing more than lip service. Even the title of the speech can be made appealing. For example, if the speech is being given to other managers, its title could be "Taking Charge of the Computer." That title will attract the attention and interest of the audience, more than a drier reference to controls.

Structuring, focusing, and even naming your speech are the big issues for every speaker. Once you have determined these, you will discover that a good part of your fear will go away. If you feel confident about what you plan to say, you will *know* you're in charge.

The fear of not being in charge as a speaker can be eliminated by deciding—at the onset—that you *are* in command of the situation. It's *your* speech and your time, and it's entirely up to you what to say. You have the opportunity to inform, enlighten, amuse, and even to inspire your audience.

Many inexperienced speakers fear hostility from the audience. Never expect hostility, since you're unlikely to experience it. As mentioned earlier, if you think your subject is controversial or likely to anger people in your audience, prepare your speech so that your comments address their point of view.

What if someone interrupts you while you're speaking and challenges your statements? It's unusual, but it does happen. The best way to handle the unexpected antagonist is to ask his or her name. Chances are, the individual won't be willing to give it. But whatever happens, you must then assert your rights. Announce that comments and questions will be welcomed once you've completed your presentation. If necessary, ask for the courtesy of being allowed to finish your talk.

Never give anyone in the audience the chance to take over. If someone disagrees with you, don't ask, "How would you handle the problem?" because he or she might just take you up on it. Then you will be out of control. The best approach is to dismiss the interruption with as little fanfare as possible, and proceed.

Some speakers prepare stock comments, just in case a heckler causes trouble. For example, a manager was addressing a group of salespeople on the subject of dealing with home office employees. During a segment dealing with bureaucracy, someone in the audience loudly challenged a statement the speaker made. The speaker commented, "I didn't realize we had someone here from the home office," and quickly continued with the speech.

You probably do not need to come up with a prepared comeback for the rare business audience heckler. Chances are, the appropriate response will come to you as long as you know your material and your audience well.

THE IMPORTANCE OF PRACTICE

When you think about practicing a speech, you probably picture some-one gesturing and talking in front of a mirror or memorizing a carefully worded phrase. That technique might work for you, but it is not necessary to practice the words and body movements you will use during your speech. You'll do better to limit practice to two areas:

1. Focus and narrow your primary message. Don't be overly con-cerned with the exact words you'll use; rather, concentrate on what you want to convey.
2. Practice the mental side of speaking. Think about your self-image, confidence, and point of view as an expert on your topic. Develop enthusiasm for your message, and build an image of yourself in control of the situation.

If you think about the environment in which you'll speak, you will realize that a certain degree of spontaneity will add a lot to your speech. You certainly want to cover the main topic and stay with an outline, and you also want to control the situation. But if you memorize a speech too well, it will be no different than giving each member of your audience a written report.

People attend live meetings to see and hear other people. They can read reports back in their own office, and they will expect more from a speaker than a reading of the message. If, during your speech, you plan to quote statistics or the words of other people, you should read those parts. However, the real message you give contains two major elements: First is the content itself; but second and of more immediate interest to the audience is your own personality. Here is your chance to include anecdotes or humor to illustrate a point, to encourage audience partici-pation, to add sympathetic statements, to inspire the audience, and to get people thinking on a topic—often a topic they thought they had no interest in, or thought they already understood completely.

You must practice your speech to some degree. But make a distinc-tion between practice and rehearsal. Too much rehearsal kills the spon-taneous elements that a lively and entertaining speech should contain. A good speech is both informative and interesting; and you can use many techniques to include both of those elements.

ORGANIZING YOUR NOTES

When we express fear of speaking, we all create an image of our fears. One of the most common of these images is that of losing our place or dropping our index cards and being unable to put them back in order.

These problems do occur during speeches, and—if they are allowed to occupy our thoughts—can add to the overall nervousness that all speakers go through. The problem can easily be avoided, however, by using a few simple techniques.

Putting a speech outline on index cards is a popular move because the cards are small, easily handled, and—perhaps the best reason of all— when your hands are shaking, index cards don't make a lot of noise. If you do use index cards, number them consecutively. Then, if you do drop them, you can get them back in the right order quickly. While rearranging your cards, break the tension with a comment to your audience. For example, say, "I did that on purpose, to keep the nervous speaker stereotype alive," or "You know, the book I read about being an effective speaker said this wouldn't happen."

Don't let the mistake overcome you. Your audience is on your side. They want you to succeed; but if you become uncomfortable, they will feel it and become uncomfortable as well. The purpose of making a comment is twofold: first, it lightens the mood and breaks the tension; and second, it gives you time to get your cards back in order.

Rather than using cards, consider writing your speech outline on a single sheet of paper and placing the paper on the podium (if one is available). Few speakers want to stand in front of a group, holding one or more sheets of paper. And having a podium is certainly a useful crutch, especially for the first-time speaker. It's not only a place to put your notes; it's also a place to hide during the first few minutes—a tool for getting through the initial terror of standing up in front of a sea of faces and making it to the actual effective delivery of the speech.

Another approach that is useful when your outline requires more space than a single page is to use a legal pad. Write your outline on the pad and leave your pages intact. Like the index cards, the pad will not show a shaking hand; and like the podium itself, it may serve as a crutch.

Many speakers have discovered that extensive notes are not necessary to the delivery of an eloquent speech. All you really need is a broad outline of the major topics you plan to cover. Keep one point in mind concerning notes: You are an expert in the subject and do not need the notes to get through the experience. The purpose of notes is only to ensure that you cover your major points.

Having an excess of notes may impede you in your attempt to communicate with the audience. If you are overly dependent on your outline, you lose both the flexibility to adjust to the audience's interests, and the relaxed and confident attitude that audiences like to see in speakers.

Some speakers concentrate almost solely on the mental part of their speech making: self-confidence, the channeling of nervous energy into a constructive and powerful force, and an intuitive understanding of the message a particular audience wants and needs to hear. They spend very little time actually outlining what they plan to say.

One speaker used this system: He usually arrived at the convention hall 30 minutes before his scheduled talk. He listened for a while to the preceding speaker, observed the audience, and made *mental* notes to himself. Then, about ten minutes before he went on, he scribbled a few notes—representing a broad outline—on a sheet of paper, an envelope, or anything else available.

His success as a speaker came not from memorizing the actual words he planned to speak, or even from using a detailed outline. He accepted the idea that he was an expert in his subject, and that he knew it well enough to deliver an interesting, informative speech. His success was derived from self-confidence, knowledge, honesty, and—most of all—his concentration on mental preparation.

Many businesspeople have a recurring difficulty in speaking to groups, even with extensive material preparation. They make the mistake of thinking that preparation relates to *what* they will say. But they spend no time working on themselves. And you must always be aware that audiences may hear what you're saying, but they're much more interested in *how* you say it.

The message a speaker delivers is a vehicle for making an impression, not for conveying information. Audiences react to a lively, entertaining speaker by retaining what was said. A boring, nervous, or uninteresting speech is rarely recalled—regardless of the actual material content.

SPEAKER AND AUDIENCE INTERACTION

Most people think that a speech is, by nature, words delivered in front of a large audience. However, you may be required to speak to a relatively small group, even to one other person. Whether your presentation is to an audience of one or to a gathering of one thousand, many of the same rules for effective speaking apply.

In some respects smaller groups are more challenging to you as a speaker. The larger your audience, the more obscure the audience personality. A very large group, by its very vastness, might make you less nervous than a small meeting room with ten attendees; or than a roundtable, where your audience is not only directly across from you, but also on both sides.

Your audience is constantly watching you. The way you move your hands, your posture, the tone of your voice, and eye contact are being judged as you speak. When you're speaking in front of a large group, you are probably not overly aware of individual responses—unless you happen to catch someone smiling at you or, on the other extreme, yawning while you deliver what you consider an inspiring message.

It's different in a one-to-one meeting. Not only is your audience judging you as you speak; you get instant feedback. The other person's responses—both verbal and physical—affect you at once and may even alter the course of your presentation.

A one-to-one presentation demands that you be more flexible, because by its nature, it is not as much a presentation as a form of direct interaction. Even though you may be doing most of the speaking, it's a dialogue, with much of the speaking taking place in nonverbal response (from the listener) and reaction to that response (by the speaker).

Five major characteristics concerning the nature of speeches differ based on the size of the group (see the chart in Figure 3-2):

1. *Interaction.* Be aware of interaction levels and the way that those levels change with the size of the audience. You will have a high degree

Figure 3-2.   Attributes by audience size.

One-to-One	Small Group	Large Group
high degree of interaction		limited or controlled interaction
speaker is aware of audience's nonverbal messages		nonverbal messages not obvious
speaker directs message to individuals		speaker addresses the entity
dialogue is natural	dialogue is limited	no dialogue
control shifts	control level varies	speaker is in control

of interaction—both verbal and nonverbal—in groups that are smaller; there is little if any interaction between a speaker and members of a large group.

2. *Nonverbal messages.* As a speaker, you will be keenly aware of the interest levels in your audience when speaking to one other person or to groups of limited size—20 or fewer people. For this reason, speaking in front of limited-size groups may prove to be more of a challenge than addressing a meeting of several hundred people. Nonverbal messages are not as obvious to you, and if you pick up a negative (such as someone

leaving during your talk), it's relatively easy to shift your attention to other, more interested members of the same audience.

3. *Focus*. With limited-size groups, your speaker's focus will be very directed. You will address messages to individuals, often in a conversational, one-on-one manner. With a larger group it's natural to consider the audience as a single entity. The entity has a singular personality of its own, yet it is not as judgmental as individuals.

4. *Dialogue*. When you speak with one person, a dialogue is natural. In fact, a presentation will invariably turn into a dialogue. The level of dialogue is more limited with a small group; and with a large group, there is no dialogue except during question-and-answer periods. And that is a restricted and controlled form of dialogue. Make a distinction between dialogue and interaction. Dialogue refers only to the direction that your speech takes. With a small group you may serve only as a mediator, and the group itself dictates the direction in which the discussion moves. With one other person the level of involvement dictates how the speech progresses, often from equal participation by presenter and listener. Interaction, however, encompasses not only dialogue but interest level as well. An effective speaker remains effective only as long as the audience is interested and involved. For that to happen, a high level of interaction is required, even when there is no dialogue.

5. *Control*. We have all been involved in a presentation to one other person. No matter how well organized its beginning, it will invariably take a direction of its own. Thus, control shifts in the one-to-one meeting between presenter and listener. In a group of limited size, especially a workshop or roundtable, control is shared, and the group is encouraged to speak up. But the speaker maintains the upper hand, deciding when to move on. In a large group the speaker has all of the control, and the audience has none. The audience is passive.

FOCUS ON THE MESSAGE

It is as important to concentrate on mental preparation as on the outline of your speech, as we have already stated. However, this does not mean that the message is unimportant. After all, you will be up there in front of those people to tell them something. So while the mental aspects of speaking can make the difference between terror and satisfaction, the content of your speech certainly must be well thought out, comprehensive, focused, and of immediate interest to the audience.

You have two points to contend with in getting ready to stand up and speak out. The most crippling fear comes from lack of mental readiness; yet the greatest effort often is directed toward the speech outline. To succeed in your speaking adventure, you must combine these two points and meld both, so that your final presentation is natural, sincere, energetic, and interesting.

Most first-time speakers are overwhelmed by being told that they have 45 minutes to fill . . . or 60 or even only 20 minutes. "What could I have to say that would take that long?" is a common immediate response. And imagine the reaction to being told that you will speak to a group for three hours.

A truly really challenging assignment is to condense a speech into a limited amount of time, without running over. And as anyone who has attended a meeting or convention knows, speakers often run too long—even, or perhaps especially, the uninteresting speakers.

Do not attempt to stretch what you consider a brief subject, just to fill up an allotted time period. If you're given an hour to deliver a speech you think will take only 15 minutes, put your fears aside. The answer is to organize your broad outline, forgetting about what you'll say and concentrating on the message itself.

Example: You are told to speak to an audience about a project you successfully completed over the past year. The purpose of the speech is to explain your approach, why it worked, and what results you achieved. From your point of view, the process was long and complicated, and you have a great deal to say about it. However, you are given only 30 minutes.

The solution to the problem is to identify—from your audience's point of view—the most interesting and significant part of your message. With the half-hour time limit in mind, what must you say about your experience that will help others? The detailed steps you went through are of no real interest to others, because those steps cannot be applied to different situations. The really interesting point is found in the approach you took to solving the problem.

You could begin your speech by summarizing exactly what you achieved. Did you eliminate a major source of cost or expense? Did you develop a new, improved operating system? Did you identify a new market for your company? Once you specify the actual result, you will bring your audience's attention to the crucial issue at hand. The next step is to explain what you did that was different from the *usual* method used in similar situations. Then you can summarize the speech by briefly describing the solutions you applied to the special problems you encountered along the way.

The same technique can be applied to any situation. An interesting process of discovery takes place when you organize your outline in an attempt to narrow and focus your message. The narrower your focus, the greater the need to organize and plan carefully—not to fill up time, but to get your message across in the limited amount of time you will have to give your speech.

Example: When you were given an assignment to describe a project you successfully completed last year, your first response was that 30 minutes of speaking time was not long enough. So you identify the main points the audience will want to hear. However, even with a narrowed focus, you may find that you could still speak for two hours. So you narrow the focus even more. By following this process to the point that the message can be capsuled into a 30-minute speech, you not only narrow the focus to the audience's interest, you also achieve a highly organized message that—because of the time restraints imposed on you—cannot be altered or improved.

In many instances information you consider essential could be abandoned without affecting the quality of your message. For example, in describing your successful project, you might believe initially that it's important to give details on the profits you created. However, in the interest of time, you decide instead to discuss the initial definition of problems and approaches in developing solutions. The degree of profits, you might discover, is of no immediate interest to the audience— especially when its members are more interested in the *process* than the actual result.

Intrinsic to this idea is the need for *interesting* information. It is not enough to cover a lot of ground in your speech; you must cover it in such a way that your audience is interested from beginning to end.

Many speakers demand a lengthy period of time because, they state, they have a lot of material to cover. But, the speech they deliver often ends up a monotonous list of points, without personality or inspiration. Of much greater interest to an audience is a well-organized but fast-moving presentation. Listeners want to believe that the speaker is addressing them directly. More to the point, each individual in the audience wants to hear a message directed right at him or her.

THE AGENDA REVIEW

As a method for understanding the interests of your audience, sit down and review the meeting's agenda. Do this well before your scheduled speaking time. This helps you to perceive your speech in the meeting's overall context.

Chances are that the meeting is structured around one central theme. A training seminar will concern itself with processes and techniques; a sales convention will present ideas for practice management or explain new products; and internal meetings will involve matters of interest to managers and employees. Within each type of meeting, your speech will hold a particular focus level of interest to the audience. Review the agenda with these questions in mind:

1. *Is the audience paying to attend?* When people pay to attend a meeting, they bring a particular attitude with them: "I want to get my money's worth." Be aware that some members of your audience might not even want to be there. They could have been ordered to attend. Both the paid and forced-attendance perspectives will affect not only how you deliver your speech, but also how it will be received.

2. *What is the audience condition?* You must determine whether the people in your audience are alert at the time you will speak, or if they're tired. If you make your presentation at the end of a long day, the audience will be tired, distracted, and hungry. Some might even leave during your speech. Prepare for this possibility, and understand that you're speaking at the end of a long day; it's not necessarily your speech that's making them leave.

3. *Will you speak before a lunch break?* If you go on just before lunch, keep in mind that the audience is thinking of leaving the hall as soon as you're done. If the previous speaker runs over, you might have

to cut short your allotted time. Speaking just before lunch is one of the worst locations on the agenda.

4. *Will you speak after a lunch break?* This position is also difficult. You must recapture the attention of a distracted group. People may be chatting even after you begin your presentation. Some attendees might linger outside the room and come in late. And on a full stomach, they will be less attentive than during midsession.

5. *Are you the keynote speaker?* If you are scheduled as the first speaker on the first day of a meeting, you have a tremendous responsibility. Your speech is expected to kick off the entire seminar or convention, to set the pace and the tone. Meeting planners expect an energetic, exciting, entertaining speech in this slot. That means more pressure on you as a speaker.

Remember: the four agenda times that present special problems are the first and the last slots of the day and the time right before and right after lunch (see Figure 3-3). Be aware of the problems associated with those times, and plan accordingly if you are scheduled in one of them.

Figure 3-3.   Agenda placement.

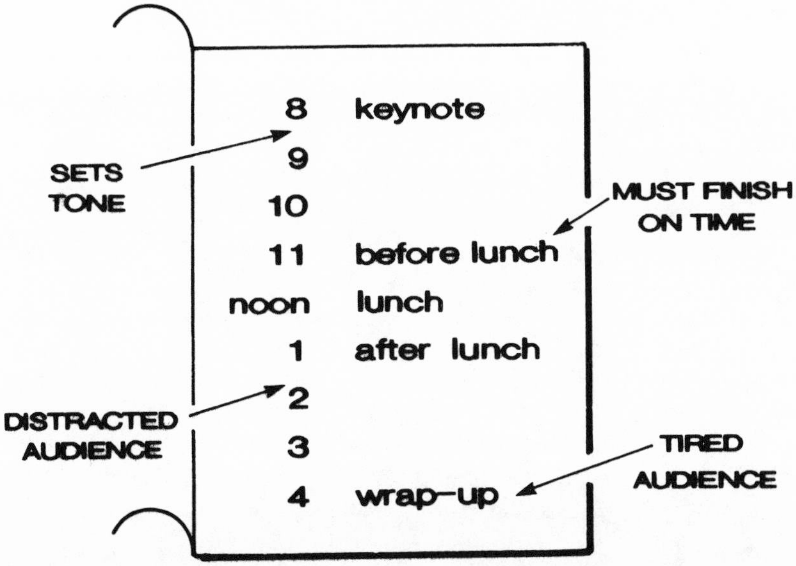

WORK PROJECT

1. You have been asked to deliver your first speech. What are three attitudes that defeat you as a speaker, and how can you counteract them?

2. In preparing for an upcoming speech, you list your outline on a sheet of paper. Name two alternatives to this note-keeping method, and describe why they might work better for you.

3. Describe the differences in control you have as a speaker when addressing one other person, a small group, and a large group. What are some of the ways you can prepare for a speech with the group size and the control factor in mind?

4

Picking Your Subject: Deciding What to Say

My duty is to speak. I have no desire to be an accomplice.

—Emile Zola

"Please don't make me give a speech," the young manager pleaded with his boss. "I wouldn't have any idea what to talk about."

"Did you know that Patrick Henry felt the same way? He suffered with stage fright, just like you and me, but he had something important to say," the boss answered. "And he was a great speaker."

"Well, that's the answer, then," the manager said. "If he's that good, let's get him to speak instead of me."

Yes, everyone does suffer from fear, stagefright, a case of nerves, or anxiety by whatever name it's given. Every new speaker confuses qualification with the simple ability to get up and speak.

The real secret is that practically no one is truly qualified to tell a roomful of people anything they do not already know or can't figure out for themselves. Great communicators may possess a special form of information they can share; but while the content of a speech is important, the real talent for speaking comes from the delivery of important material, and not just from the material itself. What talented speakers do well is convey a sense of confidence and knowledge. And while the people in the audience want information that will improve their skills, they will only respond when the delivery is good.

Some speakers are gifted at taking complex information and presenting it in a clear manner. That's nothing more than the gift of being able to organize thought and to convey it confidently and skillfully. If you analyze the good speeches you've heard, you will find that the majority of them were not involved with *new* ideas, or even particularly with educating the audience. They were case studies of clear communication, dealing with simple, basic themes we all know and grasp readily.

Think for a moment about the best speech you ever heard. Chances are that you felt enlightened, your opinions or point of view were changed, and you probably envied the speaker's simple ability to stand in front of a group. Next, think about the subject of the speech. It probably was not a complex idea, and the arguments were entirely logical and sensible—information you could readily accept because, intelligently, you already knew it. Or the speaker gave you a new perspective on a subject you thought you already knew.

Good speakers organize logic and present it in a clear manner, so that issues are clarified and arranged for you. As a member of an audience, you are allowed to perceive something that is true and that applies to you directly, but in a new light. The delivery is made in an even, concise manner, and chances are that the speech is entertaining as well. That's what public speaking is all about.

THE PROPER EQUATION

You are an expert on a vast number of subjects, most of which have never occurred to you. Abandon the common misconception about expertise and adopt a more realistic one, and you will see that being an "expert" speaker means nothing more than being able to express yourself with clarity.

The common notion is that an expert has some special or secret knowledge that most of us do not have. By virtue of education, experience, or special talent, experts have somehow attained a status that most people can never expect to achieve. Of course, this notion is somewhat encouraged by the experts of the world. But honest people—experts and nonexperts alike—know that the truth is much plainer: You are automatically granted the status of "expert" the moment that you are asked to give a speech. You would not be invited to speak unless you were considered an expert to begin with. So accept the belief and make it your own.

We are all experts because we each deal with problems and assignments in a unique manner. No two people are the same, and we each carry around our own set of priorities, our own perceptions of issues, and our own opinions about how problems should be solved. Philosophically, we are all individuals, even when we conform to common beliefs. No two people see things in precisely the same way; so even when you address a group well versed in your topic, you can bring something of value to the group by offering a new perspective. To expertly speak on your topic, you need to bridge only one small gap:

You need to identify the simplest way to convey a discussion of your expertise in a manner that a particular audience will find interesting and informative.

Several examples of this point illustrate that, indeed, the business world is made up of experts, each existing at different levels in corporations, and each having something to say to members of other levels. Some examples follow:

1. The manager of a files department spoke before an audience of senior executives, on the subject of communication between different rank levels. The value of her insights was in giving the audience a point of view that many had not appreciated or understood before the speech.

2. An accountant addressed a seminar of salespeople on the topic of record-keeping. The title of the speech was "How to Speed Up Expense Reimbursements." Even though the topic related to accounting, it was expressed in terms of interest to the audience.

3. A self-made millionaire spoke before a group of entry-level employees on the subject of success. However, he did not tell them how to amass a fortune. Instead, he spoke about career and personal planning.

All of these examples have one thing in common. They were each tailored to the group that was being addressed. If there is any "secret" to success as a speaker, this is it: You must understand your audience.

Unfortunately, many speakers are lined up strictly by topic. A meeting planner arranges a number of outside speakers, each selected on the basis of what they usually present to a group. Little if any planning is done from the point of view of the listeners and what they need and want to hear.

The basic error in this approach is structuring the program around the speakers one is able to commit. Even when there is a stated theme to a program, it is stretched to facilitate the speakers. But the audience has difficulty finding a focus to the meeting; and when you find yourself on such a program, your speaking job is made that much more difficult.

How often have you seen or heard of this happening? Someone very impressed with a particular speaker recommends that the same speaker be included in another program. The deal is put together, and the highly praised speaker is a big flop. This happens repeatedly because both planners and speakers often miss the point. An agenda cannot be put together in a vacuum, no matter how capable the speakers, unless the audience is considered as well. A good number of meetings are planned in the following sequence:

1. The time and place are decided and committed.
2. The agenda is arranged along a theme.
3. The audience is invited, with the major speakers announced.

The problem with this sequence is that the audience is left to the end, almost as an afterthought, as the assumed part of the equation. A more practical approach considers the audience as a primary factor in the equation and then aligns the perceived theme and audience and finally matches topics and speakers. When this equation is used, a program is more likely to succeed, and the speakers will be given a warmer reception—because the emphasis is placed on what the listeners need and want to hear. And since these listeners usually pay for the right to attend, a successful program must address their needs.

A general exception to this rule is the formula seminar presented by a group of professionals. For example, you receive an advertisement in the mail for a time management seminar. The speakers are announced, and their range of topics is identical in a series of programs presented around the country. These speeches never vary because they are set in advance. However, in one important sense, they *are* structured with a specific audience in mind. That audience is targeted by selective mailings. For instance, a mailing list of middle managers or executives is chosen, and the seminar's theme is aimed directly at them.

Formula meetings often are the smoothest, because they have to be. Attendees pay to attend and they expect results. And the seminar content has been tested and modified so that the formula delivers what it promises. If this was not the case, the program would not succeed.

That's a scientific way of targeting a range of topics to one audience, but it will not apply to most of the situations you will face. It's more likely that you will be asked to give a speech in a specific setting, on a specific topic, and to an audience over which you have no control whatsoever. The volatility of these factors makes it necessary for you to put considerable effort into defining your audience before you decide how to arrange and present your speech.

Example: The manager of an insurance company's policy-owner service department was given the assignment of speaking at a sales orientation seminar. The speech was supposed to be on the subject of the department's task within the company. The manager would never have chosen to speak before this group, on the assumption that he had nothing to say to newly hired salespeople. But in considering the audience, he decided to emphasize one major point: The department existed to serve customers, as a sales tool. He told the audience how to refer customers to the department and what types of questions the department staff could answer.

In this case the speaker had no control over the audience, the broad subject of the speech, or the environment. However, by considering who would be listening, he was able to construct a valuable outline.

THE AUDIENCE LINK

To say that you are an expert is not just a positive thinking gimmick, although a good, strong ego is a definite plus for a speaker. In fact, you are an expert if you can link your subject to your audience.

You might suppose that some speakers are definitely mismatched for a particular audience. But that's rarely the case. A successful speaker knows one thing better than any other: how to identify the attributes of the audience. The effective speaker knows why the people in the audience are there and what they hope to come away with. He or she then steps up to the podium and delivers exactly what the audience wants.

From the audience's point of view, a good speaker might be described as "likable." Favorable comments usually include something along the lines of "I liked that speaker more than any of the others." What this is really saying is that the speaker did a good job of touching the audience directly. Try this: The next time you hear someone express approval of a speaker, ask why. Most people will have a problem specifically telling you what it was they liked and will respond by saying, "He kept me interested," or "He was entertaining," or "He made the audience laugh."

Next, ask the question "What was the subject of the speech? There's a very good chance that the person will not even remember or will give you a vague answer. You should find it very interesting to see *how* members of an audience judge speakers. Their judgment is usually formed on the basis of delivery and impression—entertainment value. While the content may have been critical to the audience, the judgment about "good" or "bad" speakers rarely has anything to do with content, and everything to do with personality, enthusiasm, and warmth— entertainment value and communication.

We are not suggesting that to be a good speaker you need only to entertain or to turn on the charm. On the contrary, the podium is a powerful opportunity for you to share a message and to accept a leadership role. In that role you can shape opinion, change minds, and truly help other people to improve their roles in business. But to best achieve these significant goals, you must first be able to establish comfort and rapport with the audience. And that's the single attribute that most speakers lack, and the least emphasized in all of the exercises that speakers go through. Instead, a lot of time is put into the outline (tricks for the surefire speech), dealing with nervousness (how to psyche yourself out), and other formulas (the speech that will never fail.)

In the real world no one speech, technique, or outline will work with every audience. We all know this on a logical level, but few of us take the time to step back and really take a look at the people sitting out there and waiting to be refreshed by an energetic sincere, enthusiastic, and knowledgeable speaker.

YOUR OWN EXPERTISE

It is fair to say that your own degree of expertise—or lack of expertise—is a secondary problem. What's of more immediate concern is your ability and willingness to communicate with the audience. In order to do that, you need to make the link between your subject and audience's interests. All that remains is to identify how to make that link.

If you can accept that premise, then the actual work on your speech outline involves research and work. You must be prepared to deliver important and tangible information to your listeners, and to identify the form of expert advice they need to hear. The amount of effort you put into developing the best outline possible is what distinguishes you as an expert speaker. It's not your background, education, or experience that necessarily make the difference on their own.

Example: A sales manager was given the task of speaking before a group of administrative managers, on the subject of successful sales techniques. His first reaction was to wonder, "Why would anyone want to include this subject in a meeting for people who never even see a customer?" But then he came up with an interesting twist. He delivered a speech with the central theme that everyone is in sales and is selling all the time. He included examples of how an administrative manager can improve communication in the office by using the sales techniques he had employed for years to sell products to customers. His point: We all have customers, even if the customer is another department. The speech was a big success.

Example: The president of a very large corporation gave a luncheon address to a group of individuals interested in starting their own small business. He usually spoke on the subject of big-company problems. However, for this group, he emphasized start-up difficulties and drew comparisons between small and large companies. His point: All businesses face the same problem of proper management and planning. The speech was received with enthusiasm.

Neither of these examples require much of a stretch. In both cases the speaker had something of direct value to share with the audience. We all make the mistake of closing our minds to the possibilities that are presented to us. At a symposium for accountants, a meeting planner assumed that the 11 speakers to be lined up would each have to possess accounting expertise equal to or greater than the average attendee. She tried to line up senior partners from the Big Eight accounting firms, regulatory agency heads, economists, and other "heavy hitters," without any luck. In desperation she expanded her possible field and ended up with a variety of speakers. Included were a personnel manager, a successful saleswoman, a management consultant, and the head of a secretarial pool. The symposium was a huge success, and the attendees gained a lot of information about points of view beyond their own limited perspectives. After the meeting it occurred to the planner that accountants would not want so spend time at a seminar listening to other accountants; they were there to learn about other points of view.

Organizers of seminars can afford to take risks by lining up seemingly unlikely speakers, but only if they can control the subject matter and the approach each speaker will take with the audience. The manager of a secretarial pool will not give accountants anything of value by telling them about his problems. However, the people in the audience will gain a great deal if they understand how that department works, and what the best ways are to get a fast turnaround on a report. So the planner who is able to coach speakers and guide them in organizing their speeches has the opportunity to put together creative and useful programs.

In most cases, however, you will be on your own as a speaker. You will be given the assignment or invited to speak, either on a predetermined subject or on a topic of your choice. Don't expect that the person who lines you up as one of several speakers will lead you through the outline of a speech. The planner is concerned with arranging the site, timing and selecting meals, ensuring that microphones, easels, screens, projectors, and other props will be in place, and reserving rooms for staff. That leaves no time to work directly with speakers on the content of their presentation.

Accept responsibility for the focus of your subject, even when a broad topic is dictated to you. If a lot of creative energy is needed to match your expertise with the audience at hand, that's one challenge you must accept and deal with.

Spend your creative energy thinking about the audience in relation to the subject. If necessary, speak to people in that field. Ask them about the problems they face dealing with people in your line of work. Ask what solutions they'd like to see. Develop a sense of *their* point of view. That's the best way to put together a winning outline.

WORK PROJECT

1. What forms of expertise do you need to succeed as a speaker? Describe how that expertise must be applied to every speech you give.

2. Name three subjects that a marketing manager can present to an audience of accountants, so that they will find points of direct interest.

3. List five topics on which you are qualified to speak for 30 minutes. Then describe how you would tailor your theme when speaking to:

   a. corporate executives

   b. a peer group

   c. college students

5

Segments of the Talk: Breaking It Down

Proper words in proper places make the definition of style.

—Jonathan Swift

Bob told Mark his strategy for an upcoming speech: "I'm going to start by telling them what I'm going to say. Then I'm going to say it. And then I'll tell them what I said."

After a pause, Mark answered, "What was that you were saying?"

The three-part speech is a cliché that many speakers have heard before. Certainly, for purely instructional purposes, repeating material three times might be a good procedure. However, telling most audiences something three times over should be left to the classroom. In the limited amount of time you'll have to speak, you should be able to develop your speech more effectively.

There is no doubt that a strong beginning and end will support the middle of your speech; and constructing an outline in three parts is virtually unavoidable. But unless you're teaching a class, avoid the advice to "tell them what you're going to say, say it, and close by telling them what you said."

The three parts of your speech serve an important and distinct purpose. The introduction should be used to get the audience focused on your theme and familiar with you. The middle—and major portion—of your speech is the presentation of material itself. And the conclusion should not go over everything you've covered; it should emphasize your main point and leave the audience with something to think about.

ORGANIZING YOUR TALK

A successful speech has several attributes, including:

1. *Simplicity*. If your subject is too complicated to explain to any audience, you have not yet put in the time to make it simple. The simple speech is appreciated by the audience, no matter what subject matter is involved.

Remember that audiences are passive. They do not want to be confronted with a complex idea and left to figure it out on their own. They are in the audience because they want you to share something with them.

2. *Brevity*. A long speech is not a good speech. To the contrary, you will find that longer speeches become boring. It is even safe to say that the longer a speaker remains at the microphone, the greater the danger that the audience will tire of the message.

You should be able to explain your message in as short a time span as possible. When you have the luxury of a long presentation slot, you can expand the message to include more than you could in a shorter speech. And if you are allowed only half an hour, you will have to work harder to do the job as briefly as possible. That forces you to edit out unnecessary points.

3. *Focus*. Too many speakers attempt to cover a range of material far beyond a single topic or angle on a topic. As a result, their speeches become rambling, disorganized monologues, and the audience drifts off in a haze of apathy.

Focus your subject matter as narrowly as possible, even if that means that secondary aspects of the issue are not raised.

4. *Awareness.* Don't forget the people in the audience. They want to hear the information you have to give them, but only if it speaks to them directly. Many speakers have one standard speech, and they deliver it to every audience they meet. That's a big mistake.

Audiences respond best to speakers who obviously understand who they are, what they do for a living, and what problems they face. There are several techniques for achieving this two-way communication in the introduction of your speech, even if your material is the same for different groups.

5. *Energy.* An energetic, enthusiastic speaker will capture the audience's attention and loyalty with little trouble. You must bring some personality to your speeches and convey enthusiasm to your listeners, through energetic presentation.

An impassioned speaker grabs the audience's attention and holds it. This does not mean you must be emotionally involved in your subject; it does mean that you hold strong opinions and are willing to share them through clear, direct communication with others.

The combination of these five attributes translates into audience acceptance, which every speaker desires and fears being without (see Figure 5-1). Any speaker who misses the point will quickly find an apathetic or even hostile audience.

Example: The speaker at a commencement began by announcing, "I'm going to try to make this the shortest speech on record." The audience, tired from sitting for hours and listening to an endless string of speeches, immediately appreciated the speaker based on his promise. Unfortunately, he rambled on for nearly an hour, saying nothing of lasting value. By the time he was through, the audience was grateful to have made it through the experience. If you promise to be brief, you'd better come through, or the audience will not respond to what you have to say.

THE BEGINNING

Every speaker's first task at the podium is to get the audience's attention in such a way that he or she will not lose it. This is probably the hardest part of the speech to develop, and many speakers have missed the mark.

Figure 5-1. Speech attributes.

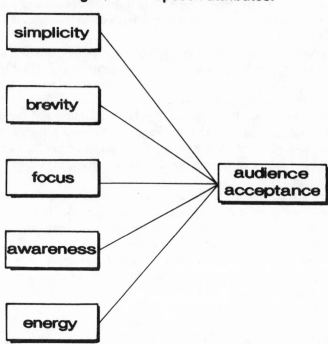

Some people assume that, just because they stand up in front of a group and begin speaking into a microphone, they automatically have the attention of the room. Don't make that mistake. You will need to start out with a statement that gets your audience's attention.

One method is to begin with humor. A brief anecdote helps break the ice, if the audience appreciates it. Even a joke may be appropriate. There are plenty of sources for funny stories and opening lines. But one critical point to remember is this: Humor will not work all of the time. The only way to be sure of its success is to devise it so that it speaks *directly* to the audience.

Example: One speaker used a standard joke that involved the often heard "three guys." In its original form, there was a doctor, a lawyer, and an accountant. The speaker substituted occupations whenever he gave a speech, replacing the three based on the occupations of people in the audience. This technique was very effective, because it spoke to the audience in a very direct way.

The one-joke speaker will eventually overuse the joke and will soon see the look of "I've heard this one before" on the faces in front of him. Jokes go out of style, so that you date your material with overuse. And remember that jokes are borrowed by other speakers. So even if you think you have a joke all to yourself, the day will come when the speaker who goes on just before you tells the joke you were planning to use. There is no simple formula for surviving the introduction. You will have to work hard to devise an opening that works, given the subject matter *and* the audience.

Most speakers will agree that humor dissolves nervousness at once. The moment the audience laughs, the speaker is at ease. But if you want to use humor and you do not trust your own spontaneity, arm yourself with several jokes, and change them as often as you can.

Another problem with humor is that it can easily be overused. Don't use humor as a way *not* to introduce your material properly. A joke or story should be very brief and used only as a bridge to the introduction you really want to use.

Example: One speaker used the transitional technique. He would tell a very brief story directed at the audience and immediately launch into his introductory material. As the laughs subsided, he would begin, "Well, just like the poor guy in the story, you all face a problem. And I'm here today to suggest some possible solutions that will make your lives easier."

If you want to open your speech with humor, it's important that you be yourself. Relate a brief experience you had that illustrates a point in a humorous way. Avoid borrowing jokes from other people, because not every story will work for everyone. The more you incorporate humor into your own experience, the better this technique will work. And as anyone who opens a speech with a joke must realize, the technique can fail. If your delivery is a little off, or if the audience is not ready for this approach, even the best joke you know could fail miserably. Chances are, rather than breaking the ice, this experience will make the task of going ahead twice as difficult.

Humor is risky. A second and much safer approach is to begin your speech with statistical information. The more startling the statistic, the better. This is similar to the journalistic hook, the attention-getting headline and first paragraph of a story that the reader cannot resist.

Speaking before a group of newly recruited insurance agents at a training and orientation meeting, the president of the company started out with the statement "There are 50 people in this audience. One year from today, only three of you will still be with the company." That certainly got the audience's attention. But after a short pause, the speaker continued, "Three years from now, two of those three will be earning one million dollars per year."

When an audience is told that only three out of 50 will make it, those oriented toward success will immediately assume they are among the three. However, this opening might be intimidating and threatening to the audience. So the president continued, "The statistics say most of you won't make it. But when each of you was recruited, we carefully selected you with the purpose of beating the statistics. And those who stay with this firm can do very well for themselves. More than anything else, I want each and every one of you to succeed."

This is an excellent way to launch the speech. By the time the introductory statement is done, the audience wants to hear every word the president has to say. Statistics used in introductions will get the audience's attention quickly, provided that those statistics have something to do with the subject of the speech and, equally as important, some affect on the audience.

Another popular introductory method is to start out with a question. Be careful with this technique. It's a popular sales trick, and you don't want your listeners to think you're patronizing them. For example, consider the tone of these questions:

1. Are any of you smart enough to know a good deal when you see it?
2. Is there anyone here who doesn't want to get rich?

Questions should intrigue the audience and not insult them. The questions above imply stupidity of failure, by their tone. They could be rephrased to compliment the audience and grab attention. For example:

1. When was the last time you saw a truly good deal?
2. Does anyone here know an easy way to get rich?

Both of these questions lead naturally to an answer, or at least into a subject—with the audience's attention well in hand. They are not insulting, and they add a very desirable flavor to your speech. The question is personal, it puts you on a one-to-one basis with each member of the audience, and it draws attention to whatever you say immediately afterward.

Regardless of whether you use anecdotes, jokes, statistics, questions, or even the promise of wealth and success, your introduction must achieve several things—before you get into the main body of your speech. These include the following:

1. *Establishing a relationship.* Your first priority must be to get on a comfortable footing with the people in your audience. You might achieve this with a joke that is tailored to them or with a statistic revealing a problem of their occupation.

Whichever technique you use, don't make the mistake of forgetting that the audience must decide whether or not to like you as a speaker. And that decision will be made in the first 60 seconds.

2. *Getting their full attention.* It's difficult to start your speech when people in the audience are talking, or if they're still coming into the room as you begin. If this is the case, don't begin to speak until you have a quiet room. And if necessary, ask the host or meeting organizer to ask for quiet before you stand up to speak.

That's the easy part. Once you have quiet, you must begin to talk, and that's when you really need to get the audience's attention. If you start out in the wrong way, you will lose the attention in a matter of seconds.

Be keenly aware of this when you plan your introduction and when you get up to talk. The worst opening is to go right into your material without saying something to start out.

3. *Explaining who you are.* In the introductory part of your speech, you must let your listeners know why you are addressing them—how you are qualified and why you have an opinion.

You certainly will not want to list your credentials in the introduction, even though some speakers have tried to start out in this way. Inform your audience within a valid context. Don't depend on an introduction from a moderator or even on extensive and detailed biographical information in the program. Remember that the audience needs a context.

Example: When speaking in front of a roomful of corporate managers, a consultant planned to discuss career planning. After an opening statement, her introduction included the statement "In the more than 20 years that I've been helping managers define their career goals . . ." This statement established experience and credibility, but it also led into an important introductory point.

4. *Summarizing a problem or issue.* The introduction must also concern itself with the reason you are speaking to the group. The best way to launch your talk is not to tell them what they're about to hear. Instead, raise the problem your listeners face. Then, in the main body of the speech, concentrate on solutions. See Figure 5-2 for a summary of these characteristics.

Proceed with your speech with an organizational structure on mind, in three parts:

Figure 5-2.   Introduction guidelines.

1. Establish a relationship with your listeners – immediately.

2. Get their full attention.

3. Explain who you are – in context.

4. Summarize a problem or issue.

1. Introduction—in which one central problem is brought up in an interesting, well-directed manner, to get and hold the audience's attention.
2. Middle—in which the one central problem is subjected to a series of solutions, or when an issue is explained in depth from a point of view that's interesting to the audience.
3. End—where the central theme is emphasized and summarized. This is not the same as "telling them what you said." It is a wrapup in which you remind the audience of the primary point you have raised and discussed.

THE MIDDLE

If you have done a precise job of organizing your material, the speech itself will succeed—that is, as long as you follow a few guidelines:

1. *Use a conversational style.* Avoid the formal speaking style, and don't lecture the members of your audience as if they know nothing about your subject. Share your experiences and observations. Don't read your speech or refer to your outline unnecessarily. Remember, you know your topic. Be comfortable with it and with your audience.

2. *Take a stand.* Use exact terms and don't hedge your opinions. And don't apologize for your position. Be secure in the statements you make to the audience, and let your confidence come across.

Replace "It might be possible for you to overcome this problem" with "You can overcome this problem." Instead of saying, "I think there might be a solution" say, "There is a solution."

3. *Avoid jargon.* Don't tell your audience that a task is "labor intensive" when what you mean is that it takes a lot of work. And when you mean "now," don't say, "at this point in time."

Be economical in the use of words, and plan your speaking style with time and interest in mind. If you can communicate your message briefly, it comes across more clearly. And if you take too much time, you will lose your audience's interest.

Let's assume that your introduction is a big success. You establish enthusiasm and energy, the people in the audience are with you all the way, and you have their full attention. Now, in the middle of your speech, you must hold their attention. That means your energy and enthusiasm must continue throughout the speech. You must continue speaking *directly* to your listeners in a conversational manner and in a way that addresses their concerns. And you must not lose the advantage you gained with a good, strong start.

Follow these guidelines for the middle segment of your speech (see Figure 5-3):

1. *Stay with the theme.* Some speakers concentrate on making their introductions powerful and interesting and then wander off during the middle portion of their speech. Getting the audience's interest and attention is only the beginning; it must be nurtured throughout the speech.

2. *Change the pace.* Be aware that your audience needs conversational variety. If you proceed through your material in a monotonous tone, you will lull your listeners to sleep. Equally dangerous is the attempt to maintain a high energy level at all times. That exhausts your audience just as much as a monotonous tone.

Use pauses, gestures, and changes in volume very selectively. But

Figure 5-3. Middle-speech guidelines.

1. Stay with the theme.
2. Change the pace.
3. Keep it flowing smoothly.
4. Include the audience.
5. Make it personal.

add enough variety in tempo and style to keep your audience interested in what you're saying.

3. *Keep it flowing smoothly.* If you will discuss several key points during your speech, move from one to another with smooth transitions. Don't jump from one topic to another. As long as you are concentrating on a well-focused theme, your points must tie together logically.

4. *Include the audience.* Some speakers isolate themselves from the audience by their style. They depend on visual aids, clever quotations, and the physical distance separating them, forgetting that the audience must remain involved in order to remain interested.

There are several ways to encourage audience involvement. Make a point and ask, "How many of you have had the same experience? Hands, please." This will vary the pace and allow the audience to help you make a point by demonstration.

Another technique is to lead the audience through an exercise. While explaining a theory of human behavior, one speaker asked each person in the audience to draw a square on a piece of paper, and then to subdivide the square into four segments. This was followed by a discussion of personalities, ending with the speaker asking everyone to decide which box he or she belonged in. This is a form of audience involvement and is much more entertaining for your listeners, who are given more to do than just sit and listen.

5. *Make it personal.* Break up the pace of your middle speech by using well-placed anecdotes or personal experiences. Don't overdo it. But you can best illustrate a key point by giving your audience an example that is personal and that they can identify with. An example with a humorous touch will further add to the entertainment value of your speech and will keep your audience interested and involved.

THE CONCLUSION

If you do your part to get and hold your listeners' attention, they will hear what you have to say. Thus, there is no need to employ the teaching method of ending by retelling what they just heard. That makes for a redundant style.

Reserve your conclusion to restate the key issue or point that you made. For example, a personnel manager spoke to fellow managers on the topic of supervision problems and their solutions. At the conclusion she emphasized a point she'd referred to several times in the middle of the speech: "No problem you face is so great that it cannot be resolved with direct, honest communication between you and the employee."

Follow these steps to end your speech effectively (see Figure 5-4):

1. *Tell the audience you're done.* If your speech concludes too suddenly, you will lose a great advantage. When you tell the people in your audience you're wrapping up your speech, you heighten their attention.

If possible, avoid the standard "in closing" or "in conclusion" wrap-up. Use other techniques to tell them you're done, such as a change in tone of voice. You may say, "Finally, I'd like to restate the central issue we discussed . . ." or "I'd like to end by emphasizing . . ."

2. *Get to the main point.* Once you signal the end, get to it immediately. Make the point and then close. Audiences like knowing when the end is upon them, but they don't want the speaker to drag it out. Your conclusion should take 30 seconds or less.

3. *End on a positive note.* No matter how great the problem you discuss, leave the audience with a sense of hope. Some problems are not easily nor quickly resolved, and the audience might have to settle for

Figure 5-4. Ending guidelines.

1. Tell the audience you're done.
2. Get to the main point.
3. End on a positive note.
4. Thank the audience.

gradual change. No matter how complex the issue, find something positive to say at the end of your speech.

4. *Thank the audience.* Be sure to give thanks to the audience at the very end of your speech. This not only sends you off warmly; it's also a matter of courtesy to those who sat and listened to you. It's also a definite, conclusive way to make your exit.

Be aware that every well-organized speech contains three distinct parts. However, if you are able to communicate on a level that the audience understands, appreciates, and relates to, you do not have to repeat any of your material. In the conclusion you can suggest actions and solutions; state the main theme emphatically; or tie the entire speech together with a final, main point.

Following this organizational plan will put the audience on your side and will help you succeed, regardless of the material or the surroundings.

WORK PROJECT

1. List two attributes of a speech that lead to audience acceptance, and describe why they are important.

2. What are two techniques you can use to get the audience's attention when you first start to speak? What are the advantages and dangers of each?

3. Name two important guidelines for staying in control and keeping the audience's attention in the middle segment of your speech.

6

The Environment: Finding Familiar Ground

I'll speak in a monstrous little voice.

—William Shakespeare

The speaker showed up early, checked the podium and microphone, and ensured himself that the room was in order. Then the audience began filtering in. He greeted each one with a smile and began assembling his notes. At 8 P.M. exactly, a man approached the podium and asked, "May I help you?" The speaker answered, "I'm giving tonight's presentation." The man shook his head and answered, "You must be looking for the room next door. This is the free speed-reading seminar."

You will succeed as a speaker if you can concentrate on your delivery, communicate your primary message, and work on attaining stage comfort. You do not need distractions. You will achieve these advantages by viewing your speaking area and the room itself well before the moment you speak.

71

Being familiar with the room, even if that means just seeing it 30 minutes before you give your speech, will make a lot of difference in your comfort level. This is especially true if you're expecting one type of room and find yourself in another. Keep those points in mind:

1. *A speech must be appropriate for the environment in which you will speak.* For example, in a very intimate setting, you can involve individual members of your audience by asking for vocal responses; participation is expected and appreciated. The same technique will not work with a large group.

2. *Your ability to comfortably address your audience may depend on what you expect, versus the room in which you find yourself.* If you're taken by surprise, you will have to struggle with the distraction surrounding you.

3. *Audiences expect varying style levels, depending on the type of room.* If you are not sensitive to this, your speech will seem out of place and will not work. You must prepare both style and content to suit the room.

THE SITE INSPECTION

To a meeting planner, a site inspection is a preliminary visit to a meeting site, with the purpose of planning meals, room bookings, speaker aids to be supplied by the hotel or convention staff, and other services. A large number of details go into this process. To you as a speaker, the inspection is more personalized and does not require as much time or effort.

An inspection may take only a few seconds, or you may want to sit for several minutes, pondering a room. You can imagine yourself at the podium, look at the speaking area from the audience's side of the room, and even stand in front of an empty hall. This all helps you to prepare yourself and places you on familiar ground. You should plan to have at least one hour to fully know the room, which includes time to listen to other speakers and size up the audience. You also will need the time to adjust your planned speech, if the room and conditions are other than what you expected.

Why is this so important? Being surprised by what you find when you are called on to speak could throw off your rhythm—to the extent that you will never be completely comfortable while speaking.

Example: A speaker had always addressed large groups from a stage. He'd always used a microphone and a podium. But when he arrived at the meeting room moments before his start time, he found the environment was much different. There was no stage. It was a very small room, in which the first row of the audience was only a few feet away. There was no podium and no microphone.

Even though the room was small, it demanded several last-second adjustments. Without a podium the speaker could not shift his weight to one foot or lean on anything; he had to concentrate on positive body language in full view of the audience. Without a microphone he had to think about projecting his voice, even in a relatively small room. And with the audience so close, he had to contend with the feeling of being crowded in.

Taken collectively, these unexpected conditions made it very difficult to deliver a speech comfortably. The speaker found he had a lot of problems to deal with, in addition to the usual nervousness.

If the speaker had arrived 15 minutes earlier, he could have observed the conditions while the previous speaker was on. He would have been able to prepare better. If he'd asked a few questions at the time the speech was arranged, some of the problems he experienced might have been reduced—if only because the element of surprise would be gone.

LEARNING THE ROOM

You may be taken by surprise due to relatively little things in a room's setup. Familiarize yourself not only with the room's environment, but with every aspect of it—even the way the seats are arranged.

One speaker had seen the room and had even delivered a speech there before. But when she arrived on the day of her talk, it was set up in theater style (seats only). She had expected classroom style (seats and tables). In addition, the podium was placed at the south end of the room; she had expected it to be at the north end.

If these details seem unimportant, think again. Anything that could throw you off must be anticipated and dealt with before you get up to speak. Consult with the meeting planner or site management to find out as much as you can, as early as possible.

Even with a thorough site inspection, you might be taken off guard. One speaker had thoroughly checked out the room in advance and even sat through other speakers' presentations. However, just before his speech, the meeting organizer took the podium and said, "Before our next speaker starts, will everyone pick up their chair and form a semicircle? That will enable all of us to interact."

Needless to say, the speaker was taken off guard. Expecting to deliver a talk to a general audience, he suddenly found himself in a roundtable format—a few moments before his speech began. By asking the right questions in advance, he could have discovered this plan and prepared for it.

Your preplanning should be done as much as possible even before you outline your speech. Knowing the environment in advance will affect what you'll say and how you will say it.

Ask these questions (see Figure 6-1):

1. *Attendance estimate.* How many people will be in attendance? Determine in advance whether you will be addressing a small group or a large group. You will need to prepare yourself based on the group's size.

Figure 6-1.   Room checklist.

1. attendance estimate

2. stage or speaker position

3. seating arrangement

4. podium and microphone

5. audience distance

2. *Stage or speaker position.* Is there a stage, or will the speech be delivered from floor level, from a banquet table, or in some other format? If you will be far removed from your audience, you will plan your speech in one format; but if the audience is at your elbow, you will have to prepare differently.

3. *Seating arrangement.* How will seats be arranged, in theater, classroom, or roundtable style? This will affect your speaking style. For example, a workshop presentation, with the audience seated at a table or in chairs arranged in a big circle, will be more interactive than a speech delivered from a stage.

4. *Podium and microphone.* Will these two speakers' props be present? They are essential when you deliver a lengthy speech from a stage. However, for less formal presentations they might not be provided. If you assume they will be there and they're not, you will have a significant adjustment to make.

5. *Audience distance.* How much distance will there be from the podium or speaking position to the first audience row? Some speakers depend on a distance of about ten feet when addressing a group of 100 or more people. If you find yourself in a smaller room with a closer, more intimate arrangement, you will be distracted.

WHERE TO FIND ANSWERS

One problem with attempting to advance-plan your speaking environment is that meeting organizers often do not have answers for you. It might prove necessary to wait until a few weeks—sometimes only days—before the actual speaking date to find out all you need to know.

Some of the problems meeting organizers face:

1. *They must line up a number of speakers and must consider scheduling conflicts, the agenda priorities, and limited time to present an entire program.*

2. *Planners rarely know far in advance how many people will attend a meeting.* They can usually supply only an estimate, based on experience with past meetings.

3. *The setup of the room—including both the seating arrangement and use of microphones and podiums—often is determined by the size of the room and the number of attendees.* So that determination might not be made until a few days before the meeting, perhaps not until hours before the meeting begins.

4. *The agenda may not be set until the last moment.* Speakers often are lined up at the last minute. So even if you are scheduled months in advance, your agenda position and speaking time are subject to last-minute changes.

These problems all present a challenge to you. While preparation is highly desirable, you must always expect the unexpected and be ready to change your format or even the time of your speech—sometimes with very little notice.

When you are asked to deliver a speech, you should depend on one primary person for answers to your questions. That person may be the meeting planner, marketing director, or chief executive of your company or of another organization. If you ask questions and get answers far ahead of the speaking date, check back before you arrive at the site to discover whether any changes have been made.

On the day of your speech, plan to arrive one hour before your start time. At the site the person on whom you have depended for answers will probably be under a lot of pressure, having to work with site management, audience members, supervisors, and staff. That person will not have a lot of time to spend with you. However, you should still expect a few minutes of orientation—especially if any changes have been made that will affect you.

Be sure and ask the questions in the section "Learning the Room." In addition, ask the following:

1. What changes have been made to the room?
2. Is my scheduled time and length of presentation the same as we discussed before?
3. Are my materials ready? (This refers to any literature that will be passed out before, during, or after your speech; overhead projection slides; charts; chalkboards; or flip charts.) Make sure that someone is there to help you organize and work with any speaker's aids you plan to use.

WATCHING OTHER SPEAKERS

Should you enter the meeting room before your scheduled time and observe other speakers? There are two points of view on this question. First, that certainty helps you familiarize yourself with the environment in which you will speak. You can observe both the speaker and the audience; you can see how well the setup works; you can note small problems, like a loud air-conditioner, which means that you'll have to project your voice to be heard. As far as getting all of your questions answered and avoiding any surprises, it does help to sit in the room and watch someone else speak before you.

However, if you are nervous about your speech, watching someone else might only intensify your fears. Because you cannot interact with people in the audience while someone else is speaking, you gain nothing by sitting among them before your scheduled time. And if entering and then leaving the room will be a distraction, it's better to avoid doing so. In a small room you will not want to draw attention away from the speaker by coming in during the talk—any more than you would want a lot of traffic taking place while you are on.

One thing you will quickly discover if you do enter the room is how noisily the door opens and closes. If it slams shut when you let go of it, the audience's attention will be drawn away from the speaker. And if the door squeaks on its hinges, the distraction will seem painfully long.

That is one of the points worth checking well before the meeting begins, if you have the opportunity to do so. If you discover a squeaking door on the meeting room, see the site manager and insist on its being corrected. That should be the job of the meeting planner; but don't simply depend on someone else to take care of all the details.

Sitting in the audience as an observer can be very beneficial or very damaging, depending on how well the audience is responding to the speaker ahead of you. One nervous first-time speaker was devastated when he quietly slipped into a meeting hall and overheard a whispered conversation in front of him. "This guy is terrible," one attendee stated. The other one answered, "Just wait. I heard the next guy is even worse."

This was the speaker's first experience in the limelight, so he knew—on a logical basis—that the statement was a fabrication. However, it was extremely damaging to his self-esteem. During his entire speech, he found his attention focused on the back of the room. At one point he saw the same two people whispering together. And of course he imagined the worst. It kept him uneasy throughout his entire speech.

DEALING WITH THE SMALL ROOM

Every speaker must contend with the problem of relating to the audience. A big part of that problem has to do with the size of the room itself.

A large room, complete with stage, microphone, podium, and a physical separation between audience and speaker, is an advantage. With reduced eye-to-eye contact and individual nonverbal messages, a speaker is able to communicate with the single entity of a large group; in a smaller group, situated in a smaller room, you must be prepared to accept a lot of individual contact.

A smaller room probably means a more interactive speech. Questions might be thrown at you during the talk; you will observe and react to individual nods and smiles—or yawns and bored expressions. All of this eye contact and awareness on your part will affect the delivery and progress of your speech.

One speaker was unprepared for a small, crowded room. He had no podium, and the first row was so close that, at one point, he tripped on the extended feet of someone in the front row. Fortunately, he didn't fall; but it did make him aware of just how close the audience was, and that fact was very distracting. He also recovered from the near-disaster with a touch of humor. As he recovered his footing, he looked back at the owner of the feet and asked, "Am I really doing that badly?"

Turn the small-room problem to your advantage. Don't let it throw you off guard, but make it a plus. See it as an opportunity to deliver a message more personally than would be possible from a stage, and with the obvious physical separation that big-room speakers enjoy and even use as a shield. Address specific points to individuals and encourage dialogue and comment from the audience.

Example: You have been asked to speak at a management seminar, on the topic of supervision. You arrive at a meeting site only to discover that you will be speaking before a group of 25 people. You will not have a podium nor a microphone, and the audience will be seated close to the front of the room. You quickly review your outline, thinking about how to deliver a speech in the new setting and how you might revise your approach to the subject. Your purpose is to create a more direct form of communication. During the speech, you revise several planned statements:

As planned for a large audience	Revised for a small group
Every supervisor has had to confront a difficult employee.	How many of you have had to confront a difficult employee?
Employees expect a number of qualities in a supervisor, such as . . .	What qualities do your employees expect from you? Any thoughts or observations?
Every supervisor I know mentions the same problem. That is . . .	You're all supervisors. What's the one thing you would like to solve?

By making your listeners a part of the speech, you attempt to draw them into the discussion. Instead of listening passively, they have an opportunity to become active participants. But there are no guarantees this will occur. At the very least they will feel more involved in your presentation. At best their participation will lead you away from the assumed outline and direct your speech more to issues that are on their minds.

These techniques usually work well in a small room, where a group will be comfortable enough to respond to the speaker on request. In a larger room individuals may be more inhibited and less likely to participate willingly. The physical separation between themselves and you, and the podium acts as blocks; the microphone gives you a verbal advantage over the people in the audience; and the stage elevates you above them. Don't try to force participation in that setting, unless you're able to walk down from the stage and into the audience yourself.

DEALING WITH THE LARGE ROOM

Larger rooms present a different set of problems. Some of these are obvious—the attributes that keep you apart from the audience, the size of the group, and the need for a microphone. While these are disadvantages to communication, they also serve to calm your nerves by keeping you separate from the audience.

You have several advantages in a large room. A primary one is that you will not be as nervous once you begin to speak, because of those attributes that separate you. And the singular, passive mentality of a large group is less threatening than a roomful of individuals.

The challenge in a large room is to communicate as effectively as you can when speaking to one other person or to a group of limited size. In the struggle with fear and nerves, an inexperienced speaker might quickly discover that it's easy to hide behind a podium, take as few chances as possible, and, essentially, ignore the audience. Many speakers deliver their material in just that way—showing little awareness of the audience or the way in which the material is being received.

If you want to become a dynamic, powerful, and effective speaker, that's not the way to go about it. Use the podium and audience separation as a shield as far as your initial nervousness is concerned. But also learn to improve your communication skills when addressing a large group. Try these techniques for improving your skills as a speaker before a large group (see Figure 6-2):

1. *If you have a detachable microphone, step away from the podium, especially when you want to make a major point and do not need your notes.*

Figure 6-2.   Improving communication skills.

1. **Step away from the podium.**

2. **Use pauses effectively.**

3. **Vary voice tempo and volume.**

4. **Leave the podium during question-and-answer sessions.**

2. *Break up your speech with a few well-placed pauses.* Excessive silence will drag the tempo of your presentation; but when you time a five-second pause well, it draws the attention of the audience to the important point you are about to make.

3. *Vary the tempo and volume of your voice, to avoid monotony in your delivery.* If you have the opportunity to record your speeches, listen and learn from you own experience. Also listen to other speakers, observing both good use of variety and the lack of it.

4. *Leave the podium during question-and-answer periods at the end of your speech.* You don't have to go into the audience, but you will communicate more effectively in this phase of your speech by standing in front of the podium or even coming down from the stage.

Do not be afraid to experiment. The time you spend in front of an audience is *your* time, and you should be willing to try new ideas. Trust your own common sense while speaking, allowing spontaneity to guide you if a more traditional approach is not working.

One speaker wore a three-piece suit on the day of his speech, but saw that most members of the audience were dressed casually. During the speech he realized that his message was not getting through, so he removed his jacket and loosened his tie. The audience responded with greater attention and interest. Whether the act of taking off his coat made all the difference cannot be known, but it certainly helped the speaker's perception.

The clothing you wear when you speak might have an effect on how the audience reacts to you. As a rule you should plan to dress well and to present your best image. In a formal convention setting, business clothing is the accepted norm for speakers; but on occasion, you will do better to identify more with what the audience is wearing.

Anything you try in an attempt to improve your relationship with the audience is worth the effort. Just be aware of how important the speaking environment is to achieving this purpose. As a speaker, you must be comfortable in the setting, or you will have to fight distractions all the way through. By investing a little time to familiarize yourself with the room, you can make the task much easier.

WORK PROJECT

1. List three questions you should ask the meeting planner at the time you're asked to give a speech.

2. You planned a formal, staged speech on the subject of politics and bureaucracy, but find yourself before a small, intimate group. To encourage interaction you want to rephrase several planned statements as questions and ask for audience response. Rewrite these statements with that purpose in mind:

    a. Everyone has experienced the frustration of trying to achieve results in a bureaucracy.

    b. There are many steps you can take to get results, even when management moves slowly.

    c. Here are some thoughts on dealing with someone who is resisting change.

3. Name two ideas for improving communication when you will speak before a large group, from a stage.

7

The Audience:
A Crowd Mentality

The time to stop talking is when the other person nods his head affirmatively but says nothing.

—Henry S. Haskins

One company that presented frequent seminars always passed out survey forms so that audience members could rate the presentation. They were asked whether future programs should be longer or shorter, whether speakers were worth hearing, and what subjects they would like to have included. One month, under the comments section, a survey form came back with the note "I enjoyed the entire presentation, but it seems no one else did. At your next seminar, please invite a better audience."

If speakers and meeting planners could control the audiences with which they worked, life would be much easier. Unfortunately the audience is the biggest unknown factor. Any given group will respond well to a speaker one time and will turn off completely another time. There is no way to predict audience reaction.

The only way to prepare well for an audience is to go to the podium with a series of assumptions that you believe to be correct. The fear that every speaker has is that of being found out. What if the people in the audience realize that you aren't qualified to speak in front of them? What if they don't accept your ideas? What if they don't respond well to you?

These fears are shared by everyone, and they are natural. However, a speaker is truly found out in these ways only when a presentation is completely offensive or inappropriate for a group—in other words, when the speaker failed to even make an effort to give the audience something of value.

THEY WANT YOU TO DO WELL

We've stated it before, but it's worth repeating: *The audience wants you to succeed.* You should think of the audience as containing only two broad classifications of people:

1. *Those who have spoken in front of a group themselves and know what you're going through, in terms of nervousness and insecurity.* Individuals in this group know all about preparation, nervousness, and the uncertainty that every speaker suffers.

2. *Those who have never spoken in front of a group and who admire anyone who can get up and survive the experience.* They believe that speaking is the most intimidating experience they could have and doubt whether they could do it well.

Both of these groups are on your side. The person who wants you to fail is rare indeed. There might be one or two misfits out there who would gain pleasure from seeing you suffer. And if you had wings, they'd gladly pull them off and watch you die a slow death. But if you consider the circumstances, you'll realize that the audience has good reasons to want only the best for you:

1. *They're at the meeting to learn from you and the other speakers.* Their time is valuable to them, so they want to gain something positive from attending. An hour goes by rapidly when an interesting and informative speaker is at the podium; but it drags on slowly when the audience is not interested.

2. *The audience as a whole is almost always sympathetic to its speakers, because the fear of standing before a group is universal.* The audience's capacity for understanding what you're experiencing and hoping for the best cannot be underestimated.

3. *Watching a nervous speaker is difficult from the audience's point of view, sometimes worse than it is for the speaker.* Few people want to sit and watch someone else suffer.

Your main competitor is yourself. You must do battle with the negative side of your personality—the side that assumes you're not qualified to speak or that you do not have an acceptable stage presence, or that no one wants to hear anything you might have to say.

The way to survive the struggle within your own mind is to develop an attitude of confidence. A confident and self-assured speaker wins the audience over—just as an uncertain and insecure speaker conveys those weaknesses as soon as he or she begins to speak. It's evident in the physical appearance and tone of voice, and in the way the message is delivered.

Example: One speaker with a doctorate degree in business confided to another speaker that being a woman was a disadvantage. "Most business audiences are predominantly male," she explained. "No one would respect anything I'd have to say without my college degree."

The attitude is completely wrong. Audiences do not decide in advance whether or not they will respect a speaker on the basis of sex, college degrees, or age. They do not check the program when a woman stands up to speak to decide whether or not she is qualified to address the group. The key to being accepted does not rest with the audience, but with the speaker.

A woman will experience a special challenge in addressing a predominantly male audience, and a man will experience a similar difficulty in front of a female group. The secret to delivering a valuable speech does not rest with any preconceived notions about you, except those you carry around in your own head.

Example: A male speaker arrived at a convention hotel to give a speech to an audience of about 300 people. When he entered the hall, he discovered that all but about five of the audience members were women. Although he realized this would be the case, he hadn't thought about it before his arrival. He was intimidated for a moment but quickly overcame the problem. He employed the technique of introducing himself to several individuals during a break. When he did get up to give his speech, he had established several audience allies. That helped overcome initial nervousness.

GETTING THEM ON YOUR SIDE

You win over an audience by speaking not in general terms, but directly and personally addressing yourself to the group in front of you. An audience of corporate executives does not want to hear about the details of a filing system or career goals for entry-level employees. And a group of secretaries is not concerned with the problems that executives deal with every day. Those topics can be addressed to an appropriate group by tailoring a theme correctly.

Example: A speaker is planning a speech about career goals. Her only experience in this field has been as a manager and, before that, as a clerical employee. How can the speech be tailored to speak directly to high-placed executives?

It's a simple matter of point of view. For example, outline topics should include:

- Developing staff incentive by helping others define their own career goals
- Training others in goal-setting techniques to improve loyalty and morale
- Techniques that help employees advance in their careers: a quality of leadership

Example: A speaker addresses an audience of clerical and secretarial employees. His topic is leadership. How can this speech be tailored to appeal to the audience? Topics should include:

- How an effective leader helps employees to advance in their careers
- How to recognize a true leader and how to train your own boss to be a better leader
- How to develop your own leadership qualities, as a method for advancing in your career

If a speech is patronizing to the audience, it will also be insulting. Thus, a speaker can never get away with talking down to the audience, whether it consists of corporate executives or filing clerks. You will get the members of the audience on your side by knowing:

- What motivates them
- What kind of information they need and want to hear
- What points of view will give them insights in matters they deal with every day

Executives, for example, might not understand that entry-level employees look to them for leadership. They might be so preoccupied with the pressures and concerns of their own careers that they've lost touch with their own employees. (In fact, that might be why they're taking time to attend the meeting where you will speak.)

If you lecture the people in your audience and tell them why they're wrong in the way they think, you will surely isolate yourself from them. But if you offer them tangible solutions to their problems, given with respect for and insight into their point of view, then you will succeed in delivering your message.

Getting the audience on your side is not a complicated process. A popular, well-received speaker does not need exceptional charismatic qualities. All that's required is an honest, sincere attempt at communication.

Every speaker starts out with the advantage that the people in the audience want him or her to do well. They want their time in the meeting to be well-spent, and they want you to give them something that's valuable, useful, and—if possible—entertaining. For the audience there's nothing as refreshing as a lively, intelligent speaker, especially if that speech occurs at the end of a day of rambling and less than interesting presentations. You can succeed in contrast to most speakers, who fail in some degree to understand their audience.

THE CIRCLE OF ENTHUSIASM

Expertise must be thought of on two separate levels. Mastery of a business subject is only the obvious prerequisite for a speaker. You have a better chance of reaching your audience when you are able to convey your enthusiasm for the topic. In that case you will have no problem gaining respect as an expert on the topic you present.

As long as you convey your message with enthusiasm, the audience will become enthusiastic as well. This assumes, of course, that you have gone to the necessary step of identifying how to best express your message for a particular group. And as the audience's sense of enthusiasm comes back to you at the podium, it bolsters your confidence and enables you to express yourself even more clearly.

This can and does occur nonverbally. Whenever a speaker begins, makes a key statement, or communicates with the audience in any manner, the reception is immediately known and sensed by everyone in the room. If the people in the audience agree with you, then you will sense their approval and encouragement.

Unfortunately, this circle works in the negative situation just as well. As soon as you make a statement that creates hostility, or when you adopt a tone of monologue that begins to bore the audience, that mood is conveyed back to you. As soon as you sense this, it is your job to take steps to reverse the trend. Skilled speakers have learned to achieve this with a well-timed pause, a change in body language, or by inter-rupting their own message to make a statement, ask a question, or jump to a different part of the outline. This ability must be developed over time and can be practiced only under the pressure of a live performance. But the skill does come, if only you will remain aware of what is going on between you and the audience.

A poor speaker is completely unaware of the circle of enthusiasm. He speaks in isolation, a passive voice spreading over a passive audience like a fog of sleeping powder. The mistake derives from the natural and purposeful separation between speaker and audience. A stage, a micro-phone, and a podium all distinguish the one person from the group. But the poor speaker makes the mistake of encouraging that separation rather than bridging it.

Average speakers might be aware of the circle of enthusiasm and might even envy other speakers' ability to manipulate it, but they don't know how to harness the circle and use it. The average speaker has inconsistent responses. One speech could be a great success, and the same delivery and message a failure in another case. "Every audience is different" is the common excuse. But that's exactly the point: *Because every audience is different, a speaker must alter the message for each occasion.*

An excellent speaker is constantly aware of the circle of enthusiasm and actually depends on it. This circle provides the focus for the speaker's control from beginning to end. He or she knows that the level of intensity must be varied, because audiences get tired of extreme enthusiasm just as quickly as they tire of a monotonous lack of energy. The skilled speaker listens to the audience's mood and senses when to turn enthusiasm levels up and down. This is like adjusting the volume on a radio: The speaker must gradually increase and then decrease enthusiasm levels and give the audience a rest with contrasting periods.

AVOIDING UNCOMFORTABLE SITUATIONS

One speaker mastered the skill of controlling enthusiasm levels, but only after several years of experience and more than 30 speeches. He had even concluded, "I'm simply not an exciting speaker." But it finally came to him that it was not his lack of ability that was preventing him from succeeding; it was his failure to control the presentation of his material.

For years he spoke on topics for which he had absolutely no enthusiasm. It was always someone else's topic, and he ended up on programs as a matter of convenience. But once he began insisting on controlling the topic and started determining *how* to deliver his message, his enthusiasm was allowed to come to the surface. He then learned how to convey that enthusiasm to his listeners—by expressing his message in terms of interest to them. You must be able to control the subjects on which you will speak. Without a basic level of comfort, you cannot expect yourself to muster up the communication skills required to succeed. Of course, you might still have a topic imposed on you. In that case find the best focus for the audience, one that you can convey with knowledge and enthusiasm.

Another approach: When you are ordered to deliver a speech and you're not comfortable with the topic, you must speak up for yourself. Negotiate, ask questions, and propose alternatives.

Example: A communications manager was instructed to deliver a speech at an annual sales convention for her company, explaining how publicity campaigns were organized and completed. She saw absolutely no connection between her job and the interests of the audience. So she approached her supervisor and brought up these doubts. Together they were able to alter the speech's title so that she discussed methods for salespeople to contribute to publicity campaigns and make the best use of publicity in their sales efforts.

In this case the manager was not asking permission to change the speech. She felt uncomfortable with it and negotiated a compromise that still provided valuable information—but that also gave her a degree of comfort she needed in order to prepare.

You might not have the freedom to change the subject or even the focus of a speech you're assigned to deliver. In that instance explain your reasons for requesting a change in the decision. Show how you propose to communicate with the people in the audience in such a way that they will benefit from hearing what you have to say.

Avoid asking for a new topic without having one or two ideas ready to offer. Approach your supervisor with alternative solutions, rather than just asking that your problem be solved.

CONFIDENCE AND KNOWLEDGE

The circle of enthusiasm is something that every speaker must learn to master. Another circle—the circle of confidence—is also at work for the business speaker.

The first time you're asked to speak, the fear factor may be overwhelming. It's a big step for anyone to stand up for the first time, even in a meeting of eight or ten executives or fellow managers. You conquer that fear with confidence, focus, and honesty and learn to survive your first speaking experience. An appreciative audience gives you needed approval, and that boosts your confidence.

You will learn to use the circle of confidence to constantly improve your speaking skills, based on the idea that confident speakers create audience approval and audience approval maintains and increases the speaker's confidence. This circle applies not only to your speaking experiences but will also improve self-esteem in every aspect of your business life. Interaction with peers, subordinates, and superiors will become more comfortable as you find yourself applying the skills you pick up under the pressure of giving a speech. You will learn to convey ideas to others with ever-increasing confidence, which may be expressed in the idea that "I did well speaking to a roomful of executives, so I can surely handle any one-on-one meeting with ease."

For example, you might be comfortable managing several employees and fielding their problems, as well as confronting peers—even handling yourself during staff meetings. But you become nervous when called into the president's office. But with success as a speaker, you will learn to interact on all levels with greater ease. It's just a matter of exposure and learning how to be comfortable and confident with yourself.

Lack of confidence is not created by outsiders. You might blame nervousness on an audience or even on one individual who holds a lot of power in your company. But in reality, those insecurities are personal and can be conquered by developing self-esteem, which comes rapidly to people who allow themselves to take advantage of opportunities to stand up in front of a roomful of strangers and give a speech. When you sense that the people in the audience are with you and that you have the power to make them think, and that you can create and control a circle of enthusiasm, you quickly discover the real meaning of confidence.

No matter what anyone tells you, and no matter how many books you read about speaking techniques, when all of the preparation is done with and all the advice is absorbed, you must still face the day when you must walk up to a podium, look out over an audience, and open your mouth to speak. Just the thought of this probably makes your stomach tighten and your mouth go dry. Don't be overly concerned. That only means you're human.

You will learn to control those feelings and convert them into energy, with a little practice. Just concentrate on your audience and on your message, and do your best to speak directly to the people listening, and you will not only survive—you will excel. As your success continues, you will find that speaking in front of others does not have to be a dreaded experience; it can be a chance to demonstrate your abilities. Success adds to your self-esteem, and you will look forward to your next speaking opportunity.

Then, as you approach the podium, and as you feel the tightness in your stomach and the dryness in your mouth, you'll be ready. You will recognize these as symptoms of energy that needs to be directed. You'll look out at your audience, and you will sense that energy as it's converted into a powerful delivery that commands the room and brings your audience to life.

SIZING UP THE GROUP

Enthusiasm and confidence make all the difference between a positive and a negative audience response. A lot of emphasis is placed on developing speech outlines, style and presentation, and other techniques for speaking—all from the speaker's point of view. Don't overlook the fact that the audience is a very important part of the equation, too. You must be able to identify what the audience needs and wants, or the best-prepared speech will go nowhere.

Judge the people in your audience and alter your speech to match them. Use these criteria (see Figure 7-1):

Figure 7-1.   Audience checklist.

1. attendance	6. economics
2. age	7. motives
3. sex	8. attitude
4. education	9. agenda
5. rank	

1. *Attendance.* The number of people in the audience will affect delivery and response. The size of your audience will dictate the approach best used.

Example: A speaker was very successful addressing an audience of 600 people. He was asked to deliver the same speech to a group of corporate employees. The setting was a corporate meeting room, and only 25 people attended. A minor alteration would have been in order: asking for audience participation, using a less formal presentation style, and preparing for face-to-face interaction.

2. *Age.* The age group of your audience determines, to a large degree, what treatment of a topic will be appropriate. Many speakers assume that groups of certain ages are interested in a limited range of topics; that isn't always true. A good, general topic, however, must be presented in a way that's appropriate to the group.

Example: A financial planner who spoke frequently addressed two groups in the same week; one was a meeting of retired people, and the other consisted of corporate employees, most in their twenties and thirties. For the first group the topic was financial planning during late-career and early-retirement years. And for the second group the planner talked about how to begin a financial plan—starting a savings program, where to find information and advice, and how to develop good investment and savings habits.

Many of the points the speaker made were identical for both groups. The difference was that the points were placed in a context that the audience would appreciate and identify with, based on their approximate ages.

3. *Sex.* A female manager had delivered a speech to a group of other women on the difficulty of supervising male employees. The president asked her to deliver the same speech to another group, and she consented. When she arrived on the day of the presentation, she discovered that the audience consisted entirely of men.

She did not change her subject or even her material. However, she did alter the message with her audience in mind. She discussed the problem in generalized terms, emphasizing the difficulties in supervising employees of the opposite sex. However, she also provided insights to many of the male managers in the audience, bringing their attention to the difficulties that women face in managerial positions. The speech was not only successful, it included an added dimension for an all-male audience.

Whenever you give a speech to an audience that is predominantly all-male or all-female, the material you deliver might have to be placed in a context you would not otherwise consider—especially if the audience is of the opposite sex.

4. *Education*. The education level of your audience is another factor to keep in mind while you deliver your speech. This refers not only to formal schooling, but also to the licensing status of the group. For example, certified public accountants do not want to sit through a lecture on bookkeeping techniques, but they might gain insight by listening to you explain the problems that bookkeepers encounter, and how CPAs can improve working relationships with their bookkeeping staff. And well-educated executives do not need advice on choosing a career path, but they might be interested in learning how they can advise young employees still in school or struggling to make a career decision.

Some speakers have experienced great difficulty, coming from the assumption that a well-educated audience will expect more from them. Don't assume that any group is too educated for you to address. You should not feel intimidated because your listeners are well schooled. Remember that they're there to hear *you* speak; you're the expert.

5. *Rank*. In addressing a business audience, you must certainly be aware of rank. A manager who is asked to speak before an audience of executives will surely experience a level of intimidation, regardless of subject matter. And an executive who is asked to speak before subordinates should be equally aware of the audience's corporate and career ranking.

Regardless of the subject, the speaker who makes the effort to present an informative and interesting speech—with the audience in mind—will succeed. However, the same caution applies here as it did regarding the audience assumed to be well educated. Don't let your audience's rank inhibit you from delivering your message as an expert.

6. *Economics*. Many speakers have failed to communicate well with an audience because they did not spend a few moments judging the economic status of the group. Financially successful people often don't stop to think that the audience members might have not yet established their own success, for example.

It would be a mistake to deliver a speech about how to shelter one million dollars in taxable income to an audience consisting of people who have trouble getting through the month without overdrawing their checking accounts, for example. And there is little point in explaining to an audience of clerical employees the best methods for managing millions of dollars in corporate assets.

7. *Motives.* Why are the people in the audience at the meeting, and what do they expect to gain from attending? This is perhaps the most important question that any speaker can ask before planning how to present material.

The approach is vastly different when people have paid $300 for the right to attend, and when they've been ordered to attend as part of their job. It also makes a difference whether you present your speech in a corporate meeting room or at an out-of-town convention.

The listeners' motives for being at the meeting will determine how they respond to the speakers. In addition, they will be motivated in other ways. Are they in attendance to learn how to make more money, to advance in their careers, to deal with employees or customers, or to fulfill a continuing education requirement? In most instances audiences as a whole share common attributes based on what they expect from attending a meeting. If you are able to identify those attributes, your speech will be directed toward meeting audience expectations, which translates into audience acceptance of your message.

8. *Attitude.* What special attitudes do the people in your audience have, and how should that affect your delivery? Be aware of attitudes toward their occupation, *your* occupation, and their position in the corporate culture.

Example: An accountant or attorney must be particularly aware that the members of the audience may make a series of assumptions, based on stereotypes they accept or believe in. The prejudice will be there and will affect the audience's acceptance or denial of the speaker's message.

Example: A female speaker addressing an audience of all-male salespeople must be aware that the audience might not accept her message as readily as she would like; thus, it must be delivered with great forethought and insight. In such a case, it is also important for the speaker to examine his or her own attitudes and prejudices before assuming too much about the audience.

9. *Agenda.* As mentioned earlier, be especially sensitive to your time and place on the agenda. You might need to modify your material based on whether you will be speaking at the beginning or end of a day, or immediately before or after the luncheon break.

It also helps if you know what subject was covered by a preceding speaker. An effective opening technique is to start with a transitional statement, referring to the previous speaker's message. Plan to use this technique when the previous speaker was especially well received and you must then follow. Every speaker knows how difficult it is to do well after an exceptionally good speaker finishes. By identifying yourself with the tone of another speaker's message, you start out on the right foot.

You have a different problem when your speech contradicts a previous speaker's message. For example, an executive gave a speech on the subject of communication. The previous speaker ended with the comment that top management is not sensitive to subordinates and does a poor job communicating. The speaker was presented with a special challenge because the audience agreed with that point of view.

The executive realized that it would be a mistake to ignore the previous speaker's remark and proceed with the planned outline when a strong opening could get the audience on his side. So he began by saying, "I agree completely that top management often fails in its mission. We do not always communicate our concern. But there are solutions, and you can make a difference."

The topic was then addressed from the point of view of the audience. The speaker pointed out ways that managers and employees could take an active part in creating an environment of effective communication. The speech was very well received, because it delivered useful information of immediate interest and use to *that* audience.

Some of the problems you might encounter with the members of your audience are derived not from their personal and demographic attributes, but from the fact that the meeting planner made a poor judgment. For example, why invite someone to speak who is entirely inappropriate for the group? Unfortunately, many speakers already know that meetings and convention agendas are often filled by people who know how to organize but do not understand the dynamics of the speaker-audience relationship. They may not even be aware of the importance of coordinating a theme.

Few experiences are as uncomfortable as having to speak outside of your own element. If your approach alienates the people in the audience, if you understand little or nothing about their careers or lives, or if you are planning to present materials that hold no interest for them, you could be heading for trouble.

The solution is to ask the right questions and to know well in advance that the audience will want to hear from you and that you have a strong, relevant message to deliver. However, if you find yourself in a situation that is uncomfortable and you realize you should not even be on the agenda, research your listeners and tailor your speech to them. You should avoid being committed to speak before the wrong group, but that is not always possible. As an employee you might be *told* to deliver a speech, a meeting planner might give you erroneous information, or you could realize at the last minute that the audience is not made up of the group you assumed you would address.

None of these problems are too difficult to overcome. But you must be prepared to alter the tone of your message so that the audience can identify with you. That objective is possible with the right amount of effort and if you ask the right questions. It helps if you have the chance to sit through a few sessions before you speak and listen to the questions audience members ask of other speakers. That tells you their concerns, interests, experience level, and what they want to get out of the meeting.

WHAT TO EXPECT

Every speaker should already know what to expect in terms of audience response, based on the nature of the audience. A common pitfall is to place too much emphasis on *what* you will say and too little emphasis on *who* it will be aimed at. We have all attended speeches that were not exercises in communication, but consisted of two entirely separate segments: a bored, restless audience on one side, and a speaker carrying on a monologue on the other. No speaker wants that situation, but many are unaware that it exists and that they have created it.

We all know that the audience is a primary element in the successful presentation. When you are scheduled to give a speech and you tell someone else about it, the first question that's usually asked is "Who will you be speaking to?" Only after that will the next question come up: "What are you going to talk about?"

When you are asked to give a speech, you probably know a lot about the people in your audience. However, regardless of how well you believe you know them, always ask these questions:

1. How many people will be there?
2. What can you tell me about the audience in terms of age, economic status, corporate rank, and education?
3. What is the theme of the meeting, and what subjects will other speakers cover?
4. Where will you place me on the agenda?
5. What will the format be? (Workshop, stage presentation, etc.)
6. How much time will I have?

Some of these questions are important not only for preparing yourself with the audience in mind, but also for self-preparation. To put together an appropriate outline, deal with nervousness, and structure your presentation to suit the audience in every respect, you must have as much advance information about the group as possible.

Your two major concerns—surviving the experience and being well received—really are one and the same. If you experience success as a speaker, your fear and insecurity will disappear. The process is self-feeding or, if ignored, self-defeating.

There are four elements of a successful speech (see Figure 7-2):

1. *Material preparation.* You must have your facts straight and be prepared to give the people in your audience information they need and value. Without this you have no reason to speak. The audience assumes that you are an expert, and expertise comes not from position, but from the willingness to work hard and to then share what you discover.

2. *Mental preparation.* Many speakers become preoccupied with their nervousness, to a degree that the other elements of successful speaking

Figure 7-2. Elements of the successful speech.

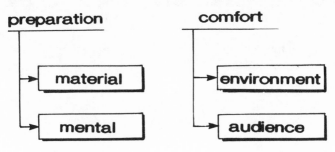

are largely ignored. However, once you understand what nervousness is, you can learn to channel it into a positive form of energy.

3. *Comfort with the environment.* You must be on comfortable ground in order to deliver a successful speech. That is achieved by studying the room, either while others are speaking or well before the program begins. It is very difficult to deliver a good speech if you are distracted by environmental problems, or if you are constantly off balance because the room is not what you expected.

4. *Comfort with the audience.* You must quickly develop a bond between yourself and the people in your audience. That is not a difficult task if you perceive their motives and attitudes, understand the demographic facts involved, and address issues that concern and affect them. Giving a speech is an enjoyable and stimulating experience if you are able to communicate honestly and sincerely, and if the listeners recognize themselves in you. That occurs when you are able to show that you understand their problems and can offer ideas for solutions.

If you work on these four elements as a singular approach to preparing yourself to give a speech, you will not only succeed—you will enjoy the experience.

WORK PROJECT

1. List two reasons why audiences want speakers to do well, and explain how those reasons can be used to prepare for your speech.

2. You are asked to give a speech on the topic of how to prepare and write a report. Your audience is made up mostly of executives. How should you modify your presentation so that it is relevant to the audience?

3. Name three criteria by which to judge an audience, and then explain how each point will influence your approach to a topic.

8

Techniques: Building Blocks to Success

Words are, of course, the most powerful drug used by mankind.

—Rudyard Kipling

"That's the last time I'll ever speak in public," a manager told his boss. "I tried to liven it up with some magic tricks, and it just didn't go over."

"Well, don't let it get to you," the boss answered. "Next time, just remember that magic doesn't work on the radio."

After delivering many speeches, you learn that some words, sentence structures, gestures, and other techniques work well and that others do not go over with the audience. In this chapter many of the successful speaking techniques are explained.

THE RHYTHM OF WORDS

You have probably noticed that some words and word combinations are awkward on paper. The same is true of the spoken word, perhaps more so. We develop our hearing and appreciation of language in a similar way to how we listen to music. Some sounds are harmonious, while others are discordant and distracting. Certain chords demand resolution, based on the rules of music that have been developed over hundreds of years. For speakers the art of putting words together is a matter of sensitivity and knowledge of the effects and rhythms of sound.

Example: Speaking style must contain a rhythm of its own. Listen to people and their use of language. A natural conversational tone is rich with variety, while a forced style is obviously distracting and unpleasant to listen to. Some speakers discover that when they talk in public they must pay extra attention to the rhythmic quality of their words.

Common practice today is to tape-record speakers at public meetings and conventions. If you have the opportunity, listen to a tape of yourself as you speak, looking for pattern flaws.

You will quickly recognize when a speaking style is flawed, but will not always know why. When something "just sounds wrong," there is invariably a reason. Below are some of the common mistakes that you should look for and avoid in your own speaking style:

1. Rhythm problems
   Example 1:
   Profit analysis is an art. Managers must be concerned with it. Profit analysis enables us to conclude. It helps us to know where we're going. It helps us to see where we've been. It helps us to know what to correct. It helps us to know what works.

   Example 2:
   Profit analysis is an art that must be of concern to every manager. It helps us to conclude, to know where we're going, and to see where we've been. It helps us to know what works and what does not.

In the first example each of the sentences contain the same rhythm. This becomes monotonous by the third sentence, and the audience immediately stops listening. It also repeats the same wording several times, beginning each static sentence with "It helps us to . . ."

The second example states the same message, but the rhythm is varied. By combining sentences into logical groups, the idea is expressed more dramatically.

2. Rambling
   Example 1:
      We have observed that when a group of managers gather in the setting of a corporate meeting, there is a tendency to conform and to accept the cultural assumptions that dominate, rather than to evaluate problems in creative and new ways.

   Example 2:
      Conformity. That's the chronic problem for the manager. We tend to conform and accept the rules in our corporate cultures. Why can we not bring our creativity to the surface to solve our problems?

   In this example a single, rambling sentence is given life with a variety of rhythm. The problem is emphasized in the single word *conformity*. The idea ends with a question, which inspires the people in the audience to put their minds to work trying to think of the best answer.

3. Hedging
   Example 1:
      It has been my observation that in some situations, managers might hesitate to act. It could be that the best solutions, or acceptable alternatives, are not always taken.

   Example 2:
      Managers hesitate to act. If you know the best solution, take it. Even if you only have an acceptable alternative, take it.

   Notice how much of the original language can be done away with or turned around. The second expression of the idea is clearer and more dramatic—action-oriented. The ending—"take it"—has punch, emphasis, and verbal drama that an audience will appreciate.

   You will have difficulty spotting problems in your own speaking patterns unless you are able to listen to a tape recording. Also listen to other speakers, and observe how they use the language.

   Self-criticism is essential here. Other people might realize that there are flaws in your speaking style, but they won't necessarily be able to tell you what those flaws are. Problems in speech patterns are not always obvious to an audience. You will have to analyze your speaking style on your own.

WORD COMBINATIONS

Some words, although completely acceptable, do not work when strung together. The uncomfortable word combination that finds its way into your speech can distract your audience for a long time after you utter it. Be aware of the rhythmic sound of your words. Most of the poorly strung words that find their way into your speech can be easily avoided with a little thought and planning.

Example: Compare the word combinations below and then study the alternatives. Look for the rhythm of sound in the words themselves, and you will realize that there are some combinations that may be described as simply wrong.

Awkward	*Alternative*
obvious objective	obvious goal
corporate cooperation	corporate teamwork
employment deployment	personnel deployment
the desks situation	the desk problem
jobs' values	value of jobs

In each of these cases, a too-similar rhythm of syllable makes the word combination distracting. Or, in some cases, words simply are not easy to hear together. For example, "the desks situation" is hard to say and equally hard to listen to. Say it out loud and you'll see why. The alternative is to change the phrase by replacing a word or turning it around. You can correct these awkward usages by simply being aware of them and looking for opportunities to correct speech patterns.

Clear communication is best achieved with short, simple words. Never feel obligated to speak at a level you assume your audience wants and expects. Be yourself. Use language with which you are comfortable. Remember, a phrase with fewer syllables will always have greater impact on your audience than a more complicated word combination.

TIPS FOR WORD USAGE

Be specific in the words you select. Edit out unnecessary words; look to your own speech pattern and simplify the way you speak. Compare these examples:

Before	*After*
management personnel	managers
at this point in time	now
liquid financial assets	money

Also be willing to take a stand without hedging your statements. Strong opinions are respected by the audience, while a hedged one is not. Examples:

Before	*After*
You might	You will
I think so	I know so
It could be possible	It is possible

Always use the active rather than the passive voice, to allow your audience to experience the life in your ideas. For example:

Before	*After*
The job must be done by us.	We must do the job.
The decision will be made by you.	You will make the decision.
Action is taken at staff level.	The staff will take action.

Try this exercise: Find one or two paragraphs in a book or memo. Study word usage. Look for opportunities to strengthen the language you hear in the ways described above. You will probably find a number of samples where the use of language could be made stronger and more vivid. Then apply the same test to your own speaking patterns.

Audiences hear only what is said to them and will not mentally add to the message. This means that the message can be only as descriptive as the speaker makes it. If you hedge your claims, qualify your main points, or add words that are not necessary, then you lose an opportunity to communicate effectively.

With a little practice, you can drastically improve your speaking style, just by being aware of the speaking patterns you have fallen into. This is especially the case for people in business. We tend to fall into the trap of communicating in business jargon among ourselves. Then, when we step up to a podium, the weaknesses in that speaking style quickly become obvious. This is one of the ironies faced by people in business audiences. In informal settings they may use jargon to the extreme, but when they're members of an audience, they expect a more eloquent, simpler style of presentation.

BODY LANGUAGE

Words may tell an audience how confidently we are able to convey information. But the way we gesture, hold our bodies, and make eye contact reveal just as much.

Extensive studies have been made of body language and what it means. Some experts claim that we all signal our insecurities, aggression, anger, and uncertainty in how we sit or stand, gesture, fold our arms and legs, and even where we look while other people are speaking to us. There is a lot of validity in the theory, although it deals in generalizations. Some examples:

1. *While a member of the audience is asking a question, the speaker takes a step back and folds his arms across his chest.* This indicates a defensive attitude.

2. *A speaker shifts from one foot to the other while delivering his speech.* The more he displays this restless behavior, the less attention the audience pays to him.

3. *The speaker makes direct eye contact with various members of the audience, making sure she directs her attention to all parts of the room.* As she emphasizes a point, she leans forward slightly, arms on the podium. This draws the audience's attention to the speaker's words and adds credibility to the message.

4. *As he steps up to the podium, the speaker distributes his weight equally on both feet, brings the microphone down slightly, and looks out at the audience for a few seconds.* All of these actions convey self-confidence.

5. *When a speaker directs her attention to different sections of the audience, she turns not just her head, but her entire body.* This sends out the message of full attention, commitment, and vitality.

All of these are examples of body language. They may be subtle, but they definitely convey an attitude. It may be positive or negative, and we often are unaware that we are sending messages at all.

Becoming aware of our own body language is necessary to add power to our overall speaking style. However, there is always the danger that, by becoming too conscious of it, our gestures and posture will become contrived.

Two suggestions:

1. *Watch videotapes of speeches you give.* Look for body language or the absence of any special emphasis. Many inexperienced speakers find themselves gripping the podium without moving at all (the "white knuckle speaker"). The complete lack of body language leaves the members of the audience feeling isolated and, as a result, they will not be interested in the speaker's message. In fact, they have the sense of not getting a message at all because they're unable to "read" the speaker. Some speakers will see obvious signaling that they will want to avoid— signs of boredom or defensiveness they don't want to send to the audience. Still others may feel that their gestures are contrived or unconvincing.

2. *Practice your body language, but only to the extent that the problems you discover from self-observation are corrected.* Avoid trying to create an impression artificially with rehearsed body language.

Don't preoccupy yourself with the message you convey, to the extent that your body language is on your mind while you speak. Simply become aware of the fact that you are constantly sending messages. Then trust your own self-confidence and enthusiasm about your material. If you feel strongly confident, your body language will convey those feelings to the audience. We tend to appear much as we feel. So the

happy, confident, self-assured speaker will naturally send out positive
signals to the audience.

GESTURES

Some speakers suggest practicing gestures in front of a mirror. Many
recommend extensive rehearsal, to the point that every move is memo-
rized, along with the exact words you will speak.

To take that approach is the same as acting in a play. The blocked-
out, premotivated thoughts and movements of the actor are practiced
for weeks in advance, to the point that the actor comes onstage as
someone else. But as a speaker, you do not want to convey an image of
a "speaker." You want to speak as yourself. That requires a human
touch, and your own personality must go through a give-and-take with
each audience. Once you begin a speech, you will discover that every
audience will react differently to you. There is no easy formula for
ensuring that one technique or another will work. Some gestures and
movements work well from a stage but will not work at all in a smaller
room. With the audience close at hand, the same gestures could be
distracting and even threatening to the audience. At the very least,
gestures in the wrong setting will take away more from your message
than they add.

A rehearsed gesture creates one impression: that of a rehearsed
gesture. You cannot deceive an audience, no matter how natural you
believe it looks. When you punch the air, sweep your arm to the side, or
make a series of pointing jabs at the audience, you may believe you are
emphasizing a point; the audience might not buy it.

Gestures should come naturally and should not be exaggerated.
Avoid preplanning them. You don't want to stand completely still while
at the podium, but that would be better than forcing yourself to go
through a series of movements that are not spontaneous. Trust in your
own energy and enthusiasm for your subject matter. Once you have
established a relationship with the people in your audience, and once
they begin accepting and liking you for what you're saying, you will be
able to relax and concentrate on delivering your message. When it comes

to gestures, the less you try, the better you will do. Let them come naturally, and they will work for you.

There are several steps you can take to give yourself a chance to vary your physical movements during a speech, especially if the microphone is not fixed to the podium. If it is attached to your shirt, for example, you have freedom of movement. Try abandoning the podium, if only for a moment. Become comfortable with the idea of stepping to one side of the stage or front of the room. Give different sections of the audience a little more attention than most speakers provide.

If you are comfortable walking around during your speech, watch out for the problem of excessive movement. While a group of managers reviewed a videotape of a convention, one speaker paced back and forth so rapidly that the scene was humorous. The camera operator had difficulty following him as he spoke. The group named that speaker the "caged tiger."

Stepping away from the podium can be used as a dramatic way to emphasize a major point, or to respond to an important question. One speaker used the following technique when someone in the audience raised a point: As he began his answer, he moved from the podium to the side of the hall where the question originated. He made eye contact with the questioner as he began speaking, then shifted his attention across the entire hall. He then continued with his answer while he walked back to the other side. He timed the end of his answer so that he was back at the podium.

Any technique can be overused, leading to a poor presentation in front of the audience. Whenever you are uncomfortable with an idea, don't try it. Let your instincts lead you. Try small, modest ideas at first and then experiment. Add dramatic emphasis to the way you state ideas. If a gesture feels right, do it. And if you are ready to step away from the podium, pry your knuckles from the sides and take the first step.

USE OF ANECDOTES

In the last chapter we briefly described the use of anecdotes in introductions and other segments of your speech. In addition to a method for establishing contact and getting attention, the anecdote is an effective technique for improving your speaking style.

Stories make speakers human. Audiences might begin listening with the assumption that the speaker's personality is of little consequence and will soon change their mind. If the speaker does well, the audience will enjoy the presentation and will like the speaker—as a person. But if the speaker performs poorly, the audience will not like the person as a speaker.

Anecdotes should never be contrived or forced. They must apply to the situation at hand—both to the material you are discussing and to the audience. For example, a speaker may plan to use an anecdote to make a point, only to realize that it didn't make the point at all. This is a sign that three common mistakes were made:

1. *The speaker assumed an anecdote would work simply because it was humorous.* This might seem a logical conclusion when you are confronting a difficult problem—as a way around the issue.

2. *The speaker believed that an anecdote would work with one audience just because it worked with another.* For example, discussing the problems of working in a small town might appeal to a big-city audience. But when you're *in* the town itself, the locals might not see any humor in the same remarks.

3. *The speaker may apply the same anecdote to different speeches.* It worked once, so it should work again. However, for the story to work, it must have a context.

An anecdote must serve as a clear example—so clear that no other way of explaining the point would work as well.

Example: A manager addressed a group of salespeople working for one organization. The president, whose name was Theo, had the reputation of being very long-winded. The subject of the speech was goal-setting as it applied both to sales and management personnel. At one point in the speech, the manager stated, "Nothing motivates you to meet your goal as well as the pressure of a deadline. Now, I know that Theo himself is up against a deadline right now, because just before I came up here to speak, he and I had a *brief* conversation."

This was an inside joke, but one that everyone in the audience understood. They had all experienced the president's "brief" conversations. Fortunately, Theo himself did not mind being made the butt of the joke.

The point here, though, is that the story serves two purposes. First, it adds to the point the speaker was trying to make. And second, it was entertaining.

Speakers do not always have positive experiences with anecdotes. Some have tried elaborate stories, only to be met with a silent, impatient audience. An analysis of the situation usually reveals that the story was inappropriate for one reason or another. The anecdote had no relevance to the talk, the speech was running over the time allowed, or it was not well delivered.

Example: A speaker addressed a men's club luncheon on the subject of paying attention and related a story from his army days: "In basic training the sergeant used to call us out by height. After 5 feet, 10 inches, he'd yell out, '5 feet, 11 inches,' and a few more men would come forward and take their places. Then he'd say, 'Now we'll see how many people are not paying attention,' and yelled out '5 feet, 12 inches.' There were always two or three men who responded as he expected."

The story went over well with that group, many of whom had been in the service and seen similar situations. However, when the speaker addressed a woman's group on the subject of supervising male subordinates, he told the same story and received a much cooler response.

Two problems with the story in that setting: First, it was not a story that most of the audience could identify with. Second, the story had absolutely nothing to do with the subject of the speech.

LANGUAGE USAGE TECHNIQUES

Be very sensitive to the three important forces at work whenever you speak:

1. Your own attitude and method of delivery
2. The material
3. The audience

These three forces must work together in order for your speech to be successful. Without the cross-current of sensitivity, the rhythm and tone of your speech will be unnatural and forced. You will know it, and so will the audience.

Anecdotes may work in the right situation and can add an important human element and conversational tone to your speech. They will help to illustrate a point, just as a good graph conveys financial information better than a column of numbers. In addition to this, learn to use language, to arrange information, and to make your point dramatically and effectively.

There are several easy-to-learn techniques that will help with this task, including:

1. *Three-point arguments.* Audiences are attracted to the grouping of three. Make use of this whenever you want to make a strong point or when you draw a conclusion.

Example: You make the following statement in your speech: "The complete computer system must have working, dependable hardware. This must be run by the right software. The third important factor is the human element—people are essential to the success of the complete system."

Now consider a revised, more dramatic way of expressing the same idea: "The complete computer system depends on three essential elements: hardware, software, and people."

Example: While explaining how the internal organization is interdependent, you make this point: "The internal staff must depend on management from above. It also depends on the loyalty of the customer base. And the third element is our vendors and other suppliers."

Or, put another way: "We in the internal staff must depend on our three essential contacts: our management, our customers, and our vendors."

2. *Two-point argument.* Another useful technique is the parallel point. This can be an expanding argument:

Example: "The solution is known once the problem is defined."

Example: "Customer loyalty grows from customer satisfaction."

The two-point argument can also be used effectively to turn a statement around:

Example: "Don't ask your company to share its profits with you; increase your company's profits and you will earn your share."

Example: "Employees will listen to you only when you begin to listen to them."

3. *Repetition.* To emphasize a point, try repeating a phrase, especially in three-part arguments. But be careful to not overuse this technique.

Example: "True leadership contains the quality of demand. It demands execution. It demands order. And it demands loyalty."

Example: "Planning cannot work without people, without time, without the plan itself."

4. *Analogy.* Add flavor to your speaking style with the use of vivid imagery. Make comparisons without too much of a stretch, and you will get the audience's immediate understanding and agreement with your point.

Example: "In some companies the creative employee is not appreciated, in spite of what management says. The last time I proposed an idea at a staff meeting, the reaction was not positive. You'd have thought I was there to steal their silverware."

Example: "We hired a young MBA who was just out of college and full of theories, and we soon regretted the decision. It was like giving the keys to the Porsche to our 15-year-old son on Saturday night."

The various techniques available to you will challenge your creativity. Practice them until they become second nature. That will happen. As you develop a level of comfort in front of audiences, you will sense the methods required to speak *directly* to the people in your audience, rather than perceiving "them" as a single, unfriendly entity.

Avoid overusing one technique that works for you. A speech loaded with analogies becomes tiring very quickly. But well-placed and carefully used techniques for effective language can add flavor and life to a speech that would otherwise be flat and uninteresting.

Compare your own response to other speakers. You can learn a great deal about effective speaking by sitting in the audience. Who did you find entertaining, enjoyable to listen to, and informative? What messages do you retain, and what messages go right by you?

Keeping in mind that the right subject matter is essential to a successful speech, the answers to these questions probably are not found in the *topic* of the speech. Rather, they are revealed by the method of delivery. Enthusiastic speakers who obviously enjoy themselves onstage will always know how to convey their message vividly through the effective use of language. The best way to become that type of speaker is to observe others who use language well.

THE IMPORTANCE OF CONCENTRATION

While you are in front of your audience, never let yourself relax too much. The moment you drop your energy level, the people in your audience will change their attitude as well. Good, effective speakers put a great deal of energy into their stage presence, and concentration is as important as it is to the actor. At the same time they are able to convey a relaxed, natural style in their delivery.

One common pitfall to watch out for when you're the member of a panel: There is a tendency to become so relaxed while the focus of attention is on another speaker that you might find yourself distracting members of the audience. One manager was in the audience during a panel discussion, but absorbed very little information. His attention was focused on one panel member who, when not speaking, spent his time picking lint from his jacket.

As long as you are "on," don't allow your attention to wander. If you are giving a speech that lasts an hour or more, you will become increasingly comfortable while in front of the audience. The danger at that point is that you will forget to feed in the energy required to make the right impression all the way to the end.

Speakers learn from observation and from experience. Become directly aware of how you speak, and think back over conversations. How could you have made your point more directly, with less qualification or hedging, or in a more vivid manner? What words do you find yourself using excessively? Was there a simpler, less complicated way to express yourself? As long as you are aware of your language, your speaking ability will continue to improve.

WORK PROJECT

1. Rewrite this sentence to improve its rhythm and impact:

> Budget development is a time-consuming process. It cannot
> be dealt with quickly or halfway. If you don't do the job thoroughly,
> there are consequences. You will pay for it throughout the year.

2. Edit these phrases to simplify the ideas and remove any
unnecessary words:

  a. It is my considered opinion . . .
  b. The appropriate management personnel . . .
  c. We depend on our staff resources . . .
  d. Anticipation precedes and creates effective execution . . .

3. Turn the following weak statements into strong, specific ones:

  a. The responsibility is ours.
  b. Timely completion is a job for the manager.
  c. Every problem cannot be solved by you.

9
Speaking Aids: Props for Communication

Human speech is like a cracked kettle on which we tap crude rhythms for
bears to dance to, while we long to make music that will melt the stars.

—Gustave Flaubert

The president of a marketing company was in the habit of
using whatever was at hand to illustrate his ideas. At one
luncheon meeting, being short of paper, he used the table-
cloth as a drawing board. After expanding the idea into a
series of flow charts and marketing checklists, he finally
called the waiter over and said, "Can you move us to
another table? This is turning out to be a two-tablecloth
plan."

We absorb most of our information visually, and speakers—in their role
as communicators—will improve their ability to convey a message with
the use of charts, slides, and other visual aids.

In this chapter we will explain the appropriate uses of speaking aids
and show how and when they should and should not be used. When
visuals help clarify your message, they can play an important role.
However, in some speaking environments, the use of visual aids will not
work. And some speakers have turned to visuals not as props for
communication, but to deal with the fear of speaking before others.

One point to keep in mind: Visual aids will improve your speech only when they are used in an appropriate way. The people in your audience will always sense whether the material you present, and the way it is presented, is applicable to them and to the environment.

COORDINATING MATERIALS

When you begin outlining your speech and deciding what to include, you can determine quickly and easily whether or not visual aids will be needed. Apply these criteria (see Figure 9-1):

1. *Is the material complex?* Whenever your subject matter is exceptionally complex, visual aids will help to clarify it for the audience. For example, a speaker explains a procedure for an audience during a training presentation. The steps are broken down into a series of explanatory flow charts. In this case visual aids are essential.

Figure 9-1.   Visual aid criteria.

1. Is the material complex?

2. Will your audience use the materials?

3. Is the material difficult to retain?

4. Will the audience need visuals?

2. *Will your audience use the materials?* If the audience will need to apply to their jobs the information you will present, visual aids will be of particular value. This is especially true if you can also include a summary for audience members to take with them.

Example: A group of newly hired salespeople hears a speech on the proper procedures for filling out and submitting completed orders. The speaker includes a series of slides, a sample filled-out contract, and a list of steps. In addition to the slides, each member of the audience is given a kit duplicating the information.

3. *Is the material difficult to retain?* Visual aids serve a worthwhile purpose when the subject of your speech is difficult to retain just by hearing. Some topics are best explained with diagrams, charts, flow charts, and other visual representations. The problem for you is determining what truly fits this standard. To make that decision, evaluate the degree of explanation required to convey your message. Can this be shortened with the use of a visual aid? Whenever the answer is yes, you can make your speech better with an overhead projection or a slide.

4. *Will the audience need visuals?* Depending on the material you will cover in your speech, the purpose for delivering it, and the reasons that the audience will be there to hear you, visual aids may or may not be appropriate.

Example: During a regional computer convention, a speaker delivers a presentation on the subject of how to select software. The speech is delivered while the exhibit hall is open, and people will attend by choice. In this case a broad overview will be given, without any detailed procedures. Visual aids will not be appropriate. The audience will not be interested in a lengthy explanation.

Example: The same speaker delivers a speech to a group of managers in a corporate training room. He is given 90 minutes, and the purpose is to give the audience the necessary steps in software selection. In this environment, and with the more focused selection of audience, visual aids are appropriate and probably required.

PLANNING THE MATERIALS

One of the dangers in using visual aids is that the successful delivery of your speech depends on adequate preparation. This means that if someone forgets to set up a projector or deliver a box of audience kits, your entire presentation is at risk.

One way to deal with this risk is to prepare your speech so that it can be completed without the visual aids. However, if you have already decided that those aids are both appropriate and necessary, expecting the worst is not a sound idea. Instead, take steps to ensure that all of the materials you will use in your speech will be on hand, without any doubt.

Speakers must always depend on other people. The site manager promises to have a flip chart on hand; a delivery service promises overnight service for a box of kits; and someone else promises to show up at the meeting with your slides. All of these plans can fall through.

If you will be giving your speech away from your own home base, you are at risk. Something essential to your speech might not be on hand at the required time. So you must be prepared to contend with problems you didn't expect. If possible, determine at least 24 hours in advance that everything you need will be in place before your time at the podium.

Example: A manager attends an out-of-town seminar and is scheduled to speak on the afternoon of the second day. When she arrives, she makes certain of the following:

1. *The home office mailed her materials that day, and they will be there the next morning* (or the materials were sent to the convention site ahead of time and are on hand).

2. *The equipment (slide projector, flip chart, drawing board, etc.) needed for the presentation is in place and ready for use.*

3. *Everything is in working order.* The slide projector is operational and the person who will be running it knows how it works.

4. *The logistics of passing out materials have been thought out ahead of time.* You do not want someone disrupting your speech by walking through the hall and handing sheets of paper to attendees, for example. It's better to have those materials in place well before the session begins.

Whenever you plan to pass out materials to the audience, make sure that this problem is planned well in advance. Request that your materials be placed in the folder each attendee receives. If they must be passed out during the session, arrange for that to be done just before you speak. Avoid having to ask for distribution of information *during* your talk.

Meet with the organizer or planner of the meeting to ensure that all visual aids and other props will be handled and prepared professionally. No matter how well you deliver your talk, poor visual aid planning makes a poor impression on your audience. And chances are that you will be blamed for the problems, even if they are beyond your control.

Example: A speaker had planned to use a series of slides to explain procedures to the audience. But as it turned out, the speaker had to run the slide projector himself, and he could not figure it out. This delayed the speech, ruined the tempo of the presentation, and irritated the audience.

Some guidelines for the use of equipment:

1. *Make sure the equipment is working before you get up to give your speech.*

2. *Make sure your information is in order.* For example, if you will be presenting a series of slides, be certain they're in the right order before you start. Number each one.

PROPER APPLICATION OF VISUAL AIDS

You may use many forms of visual aid in delivering your speech, all depending on the environment, subject matter, purpose of the meeting, and the audience.

The environment is the first component to study. If you plan to use overhead projection or slides, for example, you will need to answer four questions:

1. *Who will turn down the lights, and at what point in your speech should this be done?* Arrange ahead of time to cue the right person, instead of having to say, "Will someone kill those lights?" Help make your presentation as smooth as possible with a little preplanning.

2. *Does the room have windows?* If so, you will have to arrange for someone to close blinds or shades shortly before the presentation segment of your talk. Avoid delays that will result if you have to wait for someone to take care of outside light before you can proceed.

3. *Is there a light at the podium?* Once the room lights have been turned down and any outside light eliminated, you will be in the dark. If you still depend on your notes to continue, you must use the podium light. Be sure you know how it operates. Make sure there is a spare bulb on hand, in case the light burns out when you turn it on. And make sure you know how to replace it. Also plan to turn on the podium light a few minutes before the room lights are turned down.

4. *Can everyone in the audience read your visuals?* In one case a speaker used slides during a speech in a small room and then tried to use them again in a larger auditorium. Unfortunately, most of the audience could not read the slides, because the lettering was too small.

When you have the opportunity, go through this portion of your speech with the person who will be assisting you, whether that person will be turning off the house lights, closing drapes, or running machinery while you speak. You might discover that the assistant does not know which switches operate the lights, or how to put an overhead in the machine so that the image is the right side up. A "dress rehearsal" will reveal most of the problems you might encounter and have not planned for. It's better to resolve these problems ahead of time if at all possible.

Example: A speaker arrived the evening before his speech and ran through a slide presentation with an assistant. They agreed on cues for moving forward to the next slide and worked out the problems of using the equipment. But during the rehearsal the speaker realized that the screen was not visible from the sides of the room. Anyone sitting on the far sides would not be able to read the slides. So he spoke to the meeting planner that evening. To solve the problem, the day's session began with a request for people sitting at the sides to move to the center of the room.

APPROPRIATE USE

You can eliminate many problems of using speaking aids by planning ahead. However, the problems you might encounter while speaking are not the greatest threats. The real danger is that you will use visuals when you really do not need them.

Many speakers have fallen into this trap. You do not need visuals in every situation. And using them when the situation clearly does not require them can destroy an otherwise good speech.

Example: One speaker started using visual aids for every speech he gave. He became so dependent on them that he convinced himself he could not survive without the prop of a slide presentation. During one speech he said, "I will now discuss the proper use of the computer." At the same time he clicked to the next slide, which read, "The proper use of the computer."

In a case that extreme, the speaking aid is obviously being overused. Avoid any use of visuals when they simply are not necessary. If you plan to pass out information to the audience, you do not need to duplicate what's on the paper with an overhead in every case.

Example: A speaker led the audience through a lengthy and tedious explanation of a detailed procedure. In addition to a 27-page outline that was included in the audience's kit, the speaker flashed overheads of each page and then read and explained every line of the outline. What was supposed to be a 30-minute talk went nearly a full hour.

An alternative would have been to pass out the materials and eliminate the overhead projection. The speaker could then discuss only the essential points, concentrating on the purpose and utilization of the procedure. By saying, "You have a detailed outline in your kit, which you can study at your own convenience," the speaker could have used his time more appropriately. Instead he wasted the audience's time with an unnecessary and pedantic explanation and put the program off schedule.

Remember that visual aids should add to your speech rather than take something away. Whenever a visual reduces your speaking role to that of narrator, you are depending too heavily on props, and for the wrong reasons.

Speakers are at their best when they convey their message through their own enthusiasm and energy, and when the audience responds to them. The big pitfall concerning visual aids occurs when the speaker uses them as a crutch. To avoid this problem, consider using visuals not as a major portion of your speech, but as a separate segment.

Example: One speaker used this technique: He made his main points in a conversational discussion with the audience. Then he stopped and presented a slide summary, during which he did not speak. He never let the visual portion run more than two minutes and always followed it with a brief verbal summary. Then he invited questions from the audience.

In this example the human element predominated, while the visual portion was an added feature.

SLIDES AND OVERHEADS

Many speakers like to use slide and overhead shows throughout their speech, and they depend heavily on a constant exposure of visual information. While a purely instructional setting might benefit from this technique, most speakers are not working in a classroom environment.

Follow these guidelines for the use of slides and overheads:

1. *Use visuals as secondary aids.* Remember that *you* should be the central focus for the people in your audience. Don't make the mistake of trying to distract them with your visual aids.

2. *Keep visuals very simple.* Set up your visual aids in a uniform manner. Keep the headings the same size, with lettering large enough to read without difficulty. And use as few words on a slide or overhead as possible.

3. *Design visuals attractively.* Use color in your visual aids. But select a few colors only, and use them uniformly. Don't overdo it. Also use

both capital and lowercase lettering, rather than all capitals, which becomes tedious after a few slides.

With the availability of VCR machines, the use of video in speeches is also on the rise. Unfortunately, this can take a lot away from your presentation. You must decide how much of your speech is truly a speech and how much is nothing more than the introduction to a tape.

One speaker used videocassette technology to the extreme. He gave a brief introduction to his topic and then ran a 20-minute videocassette of himself looking directly into the camera and explaining his topic. This is an example of completely inappropriate use. Audiences prefer to hear live presentations. They come to meetings to see and hear real people, not films or excessive visual representations.

Video is a valuable medium for communication in a somewhat personalized manner. It contains more personality than a letter. But remember that a speech is only really a speech when you're there—in person.

EVALUATING YOUR REASONS

It is unfortunate for many audiences that speakers often use visuals to draw attention away from themselves. A second problem is that, with the efficient availability of computer-generated graphics in the form of transparencies, speakers sometimes think they can dazzle an audience with an attractive show.

Never use visuals just because they are available to you or because you want to make an impressive showing. The visuals you use *must* be relevant and necessary to your speech, or the audience will not appreciate them. Also avoid using visuals to take up time. One speaker was given the assignment of presenting a topic for a full hour and could only come up with a 30-minute outline. He filled in the difference with an extensive and time-consuming use of overheads. As a result, the audience was bored by the repetition and unnecessary exposure to twice the material.

There are many advantages to using visuals when they help convey your message or give the listeners valuable information. During a long session visual aids add variety to your presentation. The audience is refreshed by a break from listening to a speaker. Visual aids also increase comprehension of the subject matter. So when you have a lot of details to explain, visual aids can work as a useful tool for improving audience comprehension and interest. During a three-hour speech, any audience will welcome a brief slide show, just to break up the passive exercise of sitting and listening to another person.

Visual aids must never be used as a crutch to defend against nervousness. Some speakers have assumed that they will be able to deal with an audience only if attention is distracted away from them to a screen or chart. But when a speaker uses this ploy, the audience is not deceived. Inappropriate visuals will only intensify the sense of nervousness and discomfort at being in front of an audience. The nervous condition must be dealt with as a separate issue, not hidden behind a visual presentation.

TIPS FOR USING SPEAKING AIDS

Never forget that when you give a speech you must remain the primary focus of the audience's attention. If audience attention is diverted to a visual aid—to a greater degree than it is to you—then your message will not get through. Speaking itself is a visual art, and you should not want to miss the opportunity to maximize the impact of your message through your own presentation.

Your sincere enthusiasm, confidence, energy, and knowledge of your subject all convey much more than any visual aid—and these powerful qualities achieve the end result much more forcefully than a chart or graph. Don't become preoccupied with visual aids to the extent that you overlook the power of your own visual impression on your audience.

Follow these tips for the use of visual aids (see Figure 9-2):

1. *Be the leader.* Remember that when you stand up to deliver your speech you are the leader. Command your audience's attention as you convey the message. Adopt the point of view that visuals and other aids are there only to help you make your point, not to command center stage.

Figure 9-2. Tips for visual aids.

1. Be the leader.
2. Always talk to the audience.
3. Remember your main message.
4. Keep it simple.
5. Rehearse ahead of time.
6. Find a good place to stand.
7. Don't overdisplay.

2. *Always talk to the audience.* Inexperienced speakers make the mistake of using visual aids as a substitute audience. Their nervousness and uncertainty lead them into the common trap of ignoring their real audience. Always address yourself directly to the members of the audience, even when they are staring at a large screen next to you.

3. *Remember your main message.* Keep visual aids in perspective. Don't forget the main reason you're up there. Too many speakers let their visual aids act as the focal point of the speech, designing their presentation around the visual portion of their time.

4. *Keep it simple.* If your visual aids are too complex to grasp immediately, don't use them—or break them down into simpler parts. A visual aid should emphasize a point, not serve as a replacement for explanation.

5. *Rehearse ahead of time.* Never trust to luck or assume that someone else knows how to turn off the lights, run the projector, or close the blinds. If you will need assistance, line it up in advance, and go through the presentation beforehand.

6. *Find a good place to stand.* If you expect the people in your audience to look at your visuals, don't stand in front of them while explaining

what your visuals mean. Always stand to the side, far enough from the projection so that all parts of the room can see the visual. If you use a blackboard or flip chart, don't position yourself so that the listeners cannot see you. You should never be out of their sight. The logistical problems you might encounter should be dealt with during your run-through, well before you actually give your speech.

7. *Don't overdisplay.* Use visuals only while explaining the point with which they deal. Don't attempt to go through portions of your speech while the visual is left in the audience's view. That's unnecessary, distracting, and makes it difficult for you to maintain the audience's full attention. If you use a flip chart, for example, flip to a blank page when you're done with the visual portion of your speech.

THE AUDIENCE KIT

Your audience will quickly tire of overused visual aids, especially if you follow a string of other speakers who have abused the use of slides, transparencies, and flip charts. You must not forget that people are there to see and hear you, not to be given a show.

Another point to remember about audiences: They like to take something tangible away with them. When you give a 90-minute speech that includes a number of overhead projections showing flow charts, checklists, and outlines, they will be overwhelmed. Those who want to keep the information must scribble furiously to keep up with your pace, and those who have little or no interest in it must sit in a dark room waiting for you to finish. Both situations are negatives for you as a speaker.

An alternative is to include all useful information in your speech in the audience kit. Prepare a folder with an outline of your talk, duplicates of all visuals you plan to use in your speech, and even additional charts, graphs, and outlines. If the material in the kit goes beyond the scope of your speech, all the better.

Example: A manager had worked for several months to develop procedures and forms for use in the field. At a training seminar he was given

30 minutes to explain the new procedures. His first outline included overheads of the new forms, each to be accompanied by an explanation. However, with a limited amount of time, he chose another approach. He devised a kit that included all of the new forms and detailed instructions for filling them out. The kit also included a complete explanation of the new procedures. His speech dealt strictly with the procedures and their purposes, and he left the last 15 minutes for questions and answers. Considering the scope of the topic, the kit approach made more sense than an excessive use of visual aids.

In a training situation visual aids are valuable, but only if supplemented with materials that audience members can take with them. While broad ideas might be retained as a result of your speech, details will be forgotten. You should plan to supply your listeners with information in written form when they need to have it later.

PREPARING VISUAL AIDS

Whenever you deliver a speech that will include any form of visual aid, plan ahead far enough in advance so that your props can be prepared professionally and completely. It's unfortunate that many speakers leave this detail until the last minute. By that time, you might not be able to get exactly what you want for the best possible presentation, and you will have to settle for less.

If you will require help from your company's art department or will have to transfer information to typed form, you certainly do not need last-minute pressure in addition to the other pressures you face as a speaker. Prepare your materials before the day of your speech, and ensure that everything you need will be on hand.

Example: A speaker arrived on the day of his speech and told the meeting planner he would need copies made of a handout for the audience. All he had was a handwritten outline that ran three pages. The meeting planner had to get an assistant to find a typewriter and photocopy machine with less than one hour's notice. Because of the last-minute pressure, there was not time to proofread copy. The handouts were delivered moments before the speaker began, and several typo-graphical errors slipped through.

Never structure your speech *around* visual aids, and never depend on them so heavily that your speech will not succeed without them. The ultimate test is whether or not your speech succeeds when the visuals you planned cannot be shown, for one reason or another. If you are still able to convey your message and give the audience something of value, even without the visuals, then you will know that your plan was appropriate.

Ensuring that every aspect of your speech goes over without a hitch will require advance planning and—in the case of visual aids—assistance and a rehearsal. Keep the visual portion of your speech in perspective, and remember that the audience is there not to see what you can show them, but to hear what *you* have to say.

WORK PROJECT

1. List three things that could go wrong with a planned slide presentation during your speech. What should you look for during a rehearsal?

2. Name two criteria for deciding whether to use visual aids during your speech, and discuss why those criteria should apply.

3. What are three useful tips to follow when working with visual aids? How do these points help you to make a better speech?

10

Special Situations: Avoiding the Pitfalls

Experience shows over and over again that there is nothing which men have less power over than the tongue.

—Baruch Spinoza

Marilyn described her convention experience to Betty, detailing a busy nightlife and social schedule. "When did you have time to sleep?" Betty asked. "It sounds as if you were on the go the whole time you were there."

"Oh, I got all the sleep I needed," Marilyn answered. "There were plenty of panel discussions on the agenda."

Meeting planners are wise to vary agenda topics and formats so that daylong sessions do not become boring and repetitive. However, some forms of presentation can easily present problems of their own. In this chapter we will discuss special situations: panel discussions, question-and-answer formats, classes, roundtables, and workshops.

The following are advantages of varying formats:

1. Interactive sessions enable audience members to participate, voice opinions, and ask questions.
2. Dividing a large group into segments gives the audience a choice. Thus, the workshop format, held for a portion of the total meeting, is often well received.

3. When an unusual format best suited to a particular subject is used, it can make the presentation more valuable to the audience members.

PANEL DISCUSSIONS: MODERATORS

A panel is a group of three or more presenters who together discuss a range of materials and then allow the audience to comment or ask questions. To keep the panel on track, control time, and handle audience participation, a moderator is also essential to the panel format.

The danger of panel formats is that, unless the moderator and the speakers are aware of the audience, the presentation can be a huge failure. In too many cases the panel members forget about the audience's needs and wants, and the session becomes a closed discussion.

Example: A panel contained three speakers. Each presented a 10-minute introductory statement followed by a 45-minute question-and-answer session. Several members of the audience realized in the first phase that all of the speakers were in agreement with one another. Their 10-minute introductions were repetitive. In addition, a panel that could not disagree offered nothing that a single speaker could not provide.

A second problem came up in the way the moderator handled questions and answers. He had each panelist respond to everyone. Some of the answers were unnecessarily long-winded, and after the first response nothing of value was added by the other two speakers. As a result, the audience ended up getting three answers to each question—all of which were the same.

An audience will gain much more information when the panel members hold opposing points of view. This does not mean that a panel should become a debate. But the audience should be exposed to controversy and be allowed to hear two different points of view, more if possible. Then the answers can be interesting, and the members of the audience have the chance to make up their own minds.

If the panelists agree on the issues under discussion, the moderator should assign questions on a rotating basis. For just about any audience, one answer to a question is always enough.

If you are asked to moderate a panel, remember that audiences enjoy fast-paced presentations. A moderator is the director of the panel session, and if you do not do your job, the audience will hold *you* responsible for the failure. As a moderator, follow these guidelines before the panel session begins (see Figure 10-1):

1. *Use a stopwatch.* Set specific time limits on speaker statements and on time allowed for giving answers to questions.

When audience members ask questions, the moderator should assign the answer to one of the panel members, unless the question is specifically directed at one of the individuals.

2. *Enforce time limits.* Be an assertive moderator, and do not give up control to a panel member. When someone reaches the time limit, interrupt him or her. Devise an easy way to signal the speakers when their time is running short. For example, a brief hand signal or a card reading "one minute" should be used.

Let everyone know—panelists as well as audience members—how much time will be allowed for an answer. Suggest to the panel members that if an answer cannot be given in that time limit, they should briefly

Figure 10-1.   Moderator guidelines.

1. Use a stopwatch.

2. Enforce time limits.

3. Announce ground rules.

4. Set up in advance.

5. Identify everyone.

6. Specify the topic.

7. Wrap up.

explain that the issue is complicated and suggest that the audience member see them after the session has ended.

3. *Announce the ground rules.* Let the panelists know well before the day of the presentation how you plan to moderate. And when you begin, let the audience know how it will work, too.

If you do not let the people in the audience know how the session will operate, they will not understand when you interrupt a speaker during an answer—and chances are good that you will have to assert yourself by doing just that. However, an audience will be on your side when you do stop a long-winded response to keep the pace moving and allow the session to end on time.

4. *Set up in advance.* Make sure that all panelists have any notes at the table, know which seat they are to occupy, and know the order in which they will address the audience. Also make sure that other props are in place, such as name cards, water pitcher and glasses, and any needed speaker aids.

5. *Identify everyone.* As you begin the panel discussion, first let the audience know who you are. Don't assume the audience does not care about your identity. The moderator is part of the panel, acting as director and controller. The audience needs to identify you as well as the speakers.

Introduce all panelists, being sure to pronounce their names correctly. Identify each person by name and credentials, keeping this segment as short as possible.

6. *Specify the topic.* Be sure to tell the audience *exactly* what the panel will discuss. Set boundaries on the topic. Make these as specific as possible so that the questions the audience will ask will not take the discussion far afield from what you intend. And if any questions are asked that are off the topic, gently say so and take another question.

7. *Wrap up.* Panel discussions invariably involve a question-and-answer session that should be the major part of the program. Thus, you should be able to end on time by choosing the cutoff point. Because you are the moderator, this is your responsibility. Leave a few moments to summarize the discussion, pointing out pivotal points that were made, issues of debate, and important conclusions. Be sure to thank the panel members—by name—for their participation.

PANEL DISCUSSIONS: SPEAKERS

The guidelines for moderators apply equally to speakers on the panel. Ultimately, the presentation must be for the benefit of the audience, a point that too many panel members overlook.

To be an appreciated, effective panelist, remember that your participation is an important part of the whole program, but it is only a part. The error that many panelists make is approaching the task from a speaker's point of view. They may be accustomed to being in control during their time in front of a group, but unaccustomed to participation at the podium. Thus, a panel discussion can turn into a conflict of egos among the panelists, with the members of the audience wondering why the panel is even there.

As a panelist, follow these guidelines (see Figure 10-2):

1. *Learn the rules.* Meet with the moderator well before the date of the presentation, and ask how the panel will operate. Ask about time limits, length of opening statements and answers to questions, and how the moderator plans to communicate time limits to panel members.

If the moderator has not thought about rules, that's a danger signal. Insist on guidelines and time limits, and suggest ways the moderator can enforce them. Also be prepared for problems, since an ill-prepared moderator cannot run the panel well.

Figure 10-2.   Panelist guidelines.

1. Learn the rules.

2. Know the panel.

3. Follow the rules.

4. Stay on the topic.

5. Prepare for the worst.

What can you do if you're asked to participate in a panel, but the moderator has not yet been selected? Some meeting planners organize a program without giving much thought to the details until the last minute. In that situation insist on the appointment of a moderator as soon as possible, perhaps before agreeing to participate.

2. *Know the panel.* Who else will be on the panel with you? If you show up at the meeting expecting to present one point of view, with other panel members in accord, you could be in for a surprise. If other panelists will challenge your point of view, be prepared to present your best case and to counterargue their point of view—both in your opening statement and in response to audience questions. Avoid being a member of a panel that does not include some controversy in both the subject and its participants.

3. *Follow the rules.* When the panel discussion begins, be sure to follow the rules set by your moderator. Respect the moderator as the person in charge of the presentation. If you are signaled that your time is up, end your statement as quickly as possible.

4. *Stay on the topic.* One common problem with panel sessions is that they do not always stay with the announced topic. In some cases this is a positive occurrence; a lively discussion with the audience can be a rewarding experience, and if that occurs, it certainly should be allowed to proceed. However, if the moderator does not control a range of issues, a panel can also deteriorate into an uninteresting and unproductive hour—or worse, two or three hours.

If an audience member asks a question outside of the announced topic or limit of topics, politely remind him or her that time is limited, and you cannot respond. Then invite the questioner to see you or another member of the panel after the session is over, for an appropriate response.

5. *Prepare for the worst.* You cannot depend on the moderator to maintain control over the session. And there is not much you can do, once the session has started, to insist on enforcement of the guidelines. That's why the ground rules should be understood by everyone in advance.

However, you might find yourself in a situation where the moderator is not in control. Another speaker might not end at the agreed-upon time, for example. In that case you have two choices. Either take it upon yourself to interrupt, or simply accept the situation and hope it ends soon.

Thorough preparation is essential for speakers, regardless of the format. By being well prepared, you will be able to handle anything that comes along.

INTERACTIVE GROUPS

Speakers addressing smaller, closer audiences must be prepared for a high degree of interaction, even for dialogue in place of a speech. This occurs in small business meetings, roundtable and workshop sessions, and class formats.

You will quickly discover whether you are in charge during your speaking time, or if someone else is running the meeting. In a corporate meeting room, where ten or fewer people may be in attendance, one person must be in charge and that might not be the speaker. If you are asked to give a presentation, the meeting coordinator or other attendees can be expected to interrupt your talk with questions, points of debate, and comments. In that situation, don't try to assert the speaker's control by asking others to hold questions and comments until you are through. You must be prepared for a discussion and not a speech.

When you are asked to head a class, roundtable discussion, or workshop, interaction should be encouraged. Those sessions are the most productive when the speaker serves as a moderating force rather than the center of attention. If you inhibit interaction, attendees will not get what they came for.

When you're given the opportunity to speak in one of these settings, make sure you communicate well with the meeting planner. Some terminology may have a different meaning than you think. For example, one speaker was asked to give a 30-minute talk at a symposium. It turned out to be a roundtable discussion. In another case a speaker was asked to head a workshop, which turned out to be a formal speech setting.

Being unprepared for the format the meeting's organizer has in mind is the same thing as not preparing at all. If you research material and write an outline only to find that your job is to moderate a discussion, you will have difficulty with the group. And if you are prepared to moderate and find that you're expected to deliver a 45-minute speech to a passive group, you will have problems filling the time.

For business meetings, follow these guidelines:

1. *Identify the leader.* If it's your meeting, prepare an agenda and time limit for each item. Be sure to stay in control of the agenda so that all of it can be included.

If someone else is the leader and you are one of the speakers, be prepared to follow the meeting's format. If you are interrupted with questions or comments, you will have to alter your presentation style; there will also be times when the focus of attention shifts away from you. Attempt to complete all the points you want to cover, but accept the possibility that this might not happen. So make your major points first.

2. *Use eye contact.* In a smaller group, your audience will be close at hand. Think of this form of speaking as a discussion rather than a formal speech, and don't waste your time writing out specific language. Instead, look directly at other members of the group and present your material informally.

3. *Be brief.* In a business meeting you will not have the luxury of time. Don't plan to elaborate on points, and avoid anecdotes, humor, and case histories. Make your points as quickly as possible; then wait for the comments or questions to take over.

The business meeting presents opportunities and problems you will not encounter in any other format. This is so because there is much more involved than simply communicating your message. You must contend with interruptions and disagreement—often very vocally and forcefully stated. You might not be able to state your entire message, because even well-structured business meetings often stray from the intended course. And most of all, meetings might be less productive than you'd like. They often serve as a political forum, depending on your corporate culture and quality of leadership.

A good deal of tact must be employed when dealing with opposite points of view. Dissent might not arise from a true difference of opinion, as much as from someone else's desire to impress the boss, get attention, or establish a level of power and influence among the management team. If you go into a meeting simply to present information, you might soon find yourself lost in the ensuing "dialogue."

When you speak before a group in a workshop, roundtable, or class setting, you must assert your position as the group leader. At the same time, encourage the highest degree of participation possible. Once that occurs, your only job is to keep the discussion going and to keep it on the right course.

Follow the guidelines listed below for interactive meetings (see Figure 10-3):

1. *Define the topic.* Begin by stating the exact topic that will be discussed. Be specific. If you leave this too general, the participants will have difficulty staying on track.

2. *Ask questions.* Individual members of the group might be hesitant about speaking out. Remember that people fear drawing attention to themselves in a group setting. So begin the dialogue by addressing questions to the participants.

3. *Keep it on track.* If comments wander away from the topic, step in to get the meeting back on track. Don't lose control of the group by letting the discussion wander from what's supposed to be covered. Your

Figure 10-3.   Interactive meeting guidelines.

1. Define the topic.

2. Ask questions.

3. Keep it on track.

4. Ask for opinion.

5. End with a summary.

job as moderator can be very limited, as long as the participants follow your lead. You may have to do a lot of work, but can still maintain a limited involvement in controlling direction.

4. *Ask for opinion.* If a participant asks you a question, give your answer, but then ask for other comments. Encourage disagreement or expansion on what you say. Effective moderation usually means you will say very little, but will constantly throw the question back at the group. Keep in mind that you are not there to give a speech as much as to ensure a continuing dialogue.

5. *End with a summary.* When time is up, you will have to take control and conclude. If you've done your moderating job correctly, this might call for a very vocal effort. You might have to interrupt an ongoing debate to get control of the situation. Allow yourself a few moments to summarize the point and to state the major points of view, problems, solutions, or actions discussed during the meeting.

Every speaker must prepare in many ways whenever facing a group, whether that group is passive or active. And whether the task involves speaking or moderating, some formats present a special challenge. Perhaps more than any other way to prepare, being ready for surprises and being flexible enough to proceed is the best ability a speaker can develop.

WORK PROJECT

1. In response to a question from the audience, one of the panelists reaches the response deadline. Name two ways that you can get the speaker to wrap up quickly.

2. You present a report at a corporate meeting where other managers and executives are in attendance. During your presentation you are interrupted several times. How can you handle this?

11

Fielding Questions: The Fear of Not Knowing

Nobody has a right to speak more clearly than he thinks.

—Alfred North Whitehead

"So, what did you think of my speech?" Jim asked. Marty answered, "It went very well until the question-and-answer segment. To tell you the truth, it seemed you weren't listening very closely to what people were saying to you." Jim smiled, nodded, and said, "Thanks for the compliment."

Good communicators are always good listeners. And good speakers demonstrate that not only by delivering their messages well, but also by listening to the audience.

Speakers listen in several ways. When you first start your speech, you will be aware of a general mood in the audience. If you're being well received, if your message is getting through, and if the audience is enjoying your presentation, you will know it—without a doubt. And if the speech is going poorly, you will know that, too.

Example: A speaker addresses an audience of managers. His main theme is that managers, as a rule, do not do their jobs well. The audience develops a hostile attitude toward the speaker and, although nothing is said, everyone in the room can sense the mood.

The successful speaker must be able to listen to and respond to the people in the audience, even when they are saying nothing. You might find yourself in a situation where the audience is responding poorly to your presentation. At that moment you have a choice: Either get through your speech the way you planned and leave as quickly as possible, or adjust your message so that it gets through.

THE UNSPOKEN QUESTIONS

When speakers think ahead to their speech, they usually think of questions and answers as a session at the end of the presentation. We will discuss the question-and-answer session later in this chapter. But first you must be aware of the questions that every audience has on its mind and that every speaker must address during a speech.

People in the audience always have a series of questions on their mind (see Figure 11-1). If you structure your message to answer these questions, you improve your chances of success. They include:

1. *Who are you, and what do you have to say?* Don't expect the people in your audience to assume that you are an authority just because you're standing up there in front of them. While they want you to deliver a successful speech, you must quickly establish your own identity and place your message in focus and in a context that has meaning for them.

Example: A speaker addressed an audience of fellow accountants on the theme of the negative image the profession suffers. His first draft of an opening read, "Accountants suffer from a negative image. There are ways you can change this perception, and I'm here to tell you some of those ways." Then he realized that this was a weak and uninteresting way to start the speech. He was able to identify the subject of his speech and himself in an entertaining manner, in two sentences: "My name is Jim Adams and I'm an accountant. They tell me the first step to a cure is to stand up and announce it publicly."

2. *How will I benefit from listening to you?* Audiences expect to learn something from what you have to say. New information, insights, a fresh point of view, or support for their opinions must come from the

Figure 11-1.   The unspoken questions.

1. Who are you, and what do you
   have to say?

2. How will I benefit from listening
   to you?

3. Are you going to talk to me
   directly?

4. Will you make it interesting?

5. Are you going to end on time?

speech you deliver. Or, if you present material that raises questions and disagreement, your speech must at least make people think.

Example: One speaker was especially nervous about addressing a group of her peers. "What could I possibly tell them that they don't already know?" was the question she could not avoid. But then she realized that her experiences were worth sharing, because everyone in the audience would be able to identify with them. So her approach was to identify several problems common to all managers and then discuss solutions that had worked for her. This answered the question on the audience's mind.

3. *Are you going to talk to me directly?* Audiences always prefer listening to speakers who communicate honestly and directly. No one enjoys being spoken at. The successful speaker makes every person in the audience feel as though he or she is being addressed individually.

You can let the audience know as soon as you begin what style you will employ for your speech. In fact, you quickly identify your style from the moment you begin to speak. Don't avoid eye contact. Pause before you start, look out directly at the audience, and deliver your first words in the most direct and conversational manner possible. If you start out with humor, statistics, or questions, think in terms of informal conversation. Don't make the common mistake of separating yourself from your audience.

4. *Will you make it interesting?* As soon as you begin to speak, you answer this very important question. The people in the audience need and want valuable information, but they rarely judge a speaker on the basis of the material covered. They invariably will rate you as a "good" or "bad" speaker based on their interest in your presentation.

Tell your listeners why your project is important to them, and let them know it's also interesting. Pose questions in the beginning of your presentation, and then answer them. Critically review your topic with the members of your audience in mind. They are the most important element in the equation, and you cannot afford to overlook the interest factor.

5. *Are you going to end on time?* This might seem a frivolous question to include. But when the audience is tired and the program is long, this becomes a very important issue.

Example: A speaker was scheduled to begin at 11 A.M., with a planned lunch break at noon. But the program was running 15 minutes late. He abandoned his planned opening and instead started out by saying, "We're behind schedule now, but I promise to end by noon. I'm sure we all want to be on time for lunch." This simple promise to sacrifice 15 minutes in consideration of the audience did more to create allies than all the humor and directness the speaker could have mustered. Of course, if you make such a promise, you *must* keep it, or you will find yourself standing before a very hostile group.

DEMONSTRATING ENTHUSIASM

As long as you are aware of the unspoken questions and can answer them in the style and content of your speech, you will succeed as a speaker in the majority of cases. However, most speakers fear the direct, spoken question from the audience more than anything else. Every speaker must deal with this fear. It is best expressed as "What if someone asks me a question that I can't answer?"

You will be able to answer audience questions as long as you know your subject and maintain your honesty with the audience. If someone does ask you a question that you simply don't have an answer to, reply, "I don't know." An honest answer is really the only choice you have. If you attempt to fake your way through by trying to appear to know, you will be spotted at once.

Never assume that the members of your audience expect you to have all of the answers. No one does. And if you assume that level of pressure, you will never be able to establish a rapport with your listeners, who will trust you only if you're completely honest with them. However, you should never let your answer simply end with "I don't know." Add one more statement: "But I'll find out and get in touch with you next week. See me after, and give me your address."

An enthusiastic speaker will inspire audiences to ask worthwhile questions. And by the same rule, when a speaker delivers a speech poorly, the members of the audience will not respond. They'll just be glad to see the speaker gone from the podium and probably will not ask any questions at all. Your own enthusiasm is critical to speaking success. Enthusiasm is contagious, and an energetic, enthusiastic speaker creates an audience with the same attributes. If you want to create a worthwhile dialogue with the people in your audience, which must include an exchange during the question-and-answer phase, plan to stimulate them. Challenge them to think. Don't try to anticipate and answer every question on your topic. Always leave enough unanswered so that your listeners can feel that they are participating in your speech.

This is one of the elements of successful speaking that many speakers overlook. In addition to believing they must have all the answers, they also attempt to raise all of the questions. Focus your speech narrowly and do a thorough job dealing with that topic. If you can achieve this, you will always get the audience thinking. Then, when you invite questions, many hands will go up. For the speaker, audience reaction during this phase of the talk is much more important than a laugh at an opening joke or applause at the end. If you can create an enthusiastic response in the form of questions, then you've done your job.

There is a pitfall worth avoiding, once you have created an enthusiastic frenzy. You might run over your time. Don't feel responsible for answering every question or for staying at the podium just because the people in your audience have a lot on their minds. End your speech on time, while the audience is still enthusiastic.

You can achieve this diplomatically. As the time limit approaches, apologize to the audience: "I'm very sorry to have to end, but our time is up. Let's take one more question."

THE SHORT ANSWER

Set a goal for yourself to answer every question as briefly as possible. If you have created a mood of great enthusiasm, the best way to lose it is by giving long answers.

If you are asked a question that you cannot address in less than two minutes, explain, "The question is too complicated to answer briefly. If you will meet with me after we're done, I'll be glad to go into more detail. For now, let me give you an abridged response."

Then mention the highlights and most critical points in your answer. Leave the details for later, and give more audience members the chance to ask their questions. The most tedious speeches—regardless of how well the speaker performed—are those involving long answers to audience questions.

Brief answers also demonstrate to the audience that you are in command of your subject. By keeping everything simple and direct, you convey the idea to the audience that nothing is too complicated to deal with in a simple and honest manner. Don't fall for the misconception that the longer the answer is, the greater its value. The exact opposite is true.

If you are asked a hostile question, a brief and honest answer is best. However, speakers often deal with hostility by giving exceptionally long answers—actually, these turn into self-serving excuses and hedges that audiences find boring. The audience respects an honest, brief answer that also conveys self-confidence in your position.

LISTENING SKILLS

It is impossible to anticipate the questions your audience will throw at you. And if your topic is a controversial one, or one that angers members of the audience, you must be prepared for some very direct—even hostile—questions.

While you cannot practice answers to unknown questions, you can identify the areas where questions are most likely to arise. Arm yourself with facts, statistics, and examples that you will not use in your speech. Save this valuable information as a backup response, to be used as answers in the question-and-answer segment of your talk.

Example: You make several statements during your speech, and at the end an audience member questions your conclusions. At that point, you respond by quoting the results of a recent survey.

Never allow yourself to be put on the defensive by a question. As long as you believe strongly in your own position, you can stay in command, but if you show any hesitation or doubt in response to a question, then you will lose the audience's respect. Admit that an issue is complex and that there are several points of view. Also admit to lack of knowledge when appropriate. But don't back down in the face of hostility from a position you stated strongly and specifically.

The essence of handling yourself well during the question-and-answer session is to listen well and carefully. Follow these guidelines (see Figure 11-2):

1. *Keep your energy level up.* Don't forget that you are still the speaker. It's easy to fall into the trap of becoming overly relaxed, thinking the speech is over. But you're still on, and the question-and-answer session might prove to be the most important part of your speech.

If you relax once the questions begin, you may be taken off guard by an especially tough question. Even worse, relaxing at this point conveys disinterest on your part to the audience, an attitude you certainly do not want to assume.

2. *Be aware of the message you convey.* Your body language, eye contact, and tone of voice convey a lot to the audience. You may be

Figure 11-2.   Question-and-answer guidelines.

1. Keep your energy level up.

2. Be aware of the message you convey.

3. Listen carefully to the full question.

4. Keep your answers simple.

5. Turn negatives into positives.

6. Respect the questioner.

aware of these during the speech, but then let down your guard when being questioned.

Example: While a member of the audience is asking his question, the speaker gathers his notes together, puts them in his coat pocket, and turns off the podium lamp—all signals that he is through. The audience then gets the unintended message that their questions are not important to the speaker. Keep your intensity during the question-and-answer session, and let the members of your audience know that you value their voice as much as you expected them to value yours.

3. *Listen carefully to the full question.* Never interrupt a questioner before the question is complete, and don't nod your head while the other person is speaking. Hold eye contact until the question is over, and then give your answer.

The exception to this rule occurs when the questioner wants to make a speech of his own. In this case an interruption is in order. But handle it diplomatically.

Example: You ask for questions, and a member of the audience begins a speech. You hold up your hand and, speaking directly into the microphone, interrupt with "I'm sorry for cutting you off. But in the interest of time, please state your question so that others also have a chance."

4. *Keep your answers simple.* Remember that the brief answer is always best. Don't repeat segments of your speech in answer to a question. Mention only the highlights.

5. *Turn negatives into positives.* If someone asks a hostile question or brings up a negative point of view, repeat the question in a positive way. Then answer with an optimistic statement. Don't allow the session to assume a negative flavor, and don't let questioners distract you from a positive tone in your message.

Example: During a speech on the subject of budgeting, you are asked, "Why do we waste so much time budgeting?" You rephrase: "You want to know how budget preparation can be made more efficient and less time-consuming."

Don't avoid hostility. Confront it and deal with it calmly. For example, during your speech, you list the errors that managers commonly make, and you propose solutions to them. One of the questions you get is "You seem to have all the answers. Have you ever made a mistake?" This is a loaded question, of course. Answering it defensively would only harm your credibility. So you calmly reply, "Yes, I've made many mistakes. That's where I got all of my experience."

6. *Respect the questioner.* Never ridicule a question or the person asking it. Treat members of the audience with respect, even when one person does not grant you the same courtesy.

Respond to hostility with very, very brief answers and then move on to the next question. Never respond by turning the question around and asking the audience member a question in response. That only gives the floor to someone you'd rather not hear from.

TURNING IT AROUND

How should you deal with the problem that arises when you invite questions and no one asks any? Should you stop ahead of schedule and get away from the podium as quickly as possible? Or are there other solutions?

If your speech goes poorly, it is not always your fault. The audience might be exhausted after a long day of sessions. The agenda might be well over schedule. And listeners might simply want to end the day and get to the cocktail party. In these instances it is best to end as quickly as you can and release the audience.

However, if your speech was well delivered, and the audience responded well, the situation is different. It may be that people don't want to raise their hand or can't think of a worthwhile question. In that case take advantage of the time remaining to create a truly interactive session.

Once you invite questions and no one responds, make the following statement: "If you don't have any questions for me, let me ask you something. How many of you here have encountered the problem we discussed? How did you deal with it?"

Ask the audience to participate. You will discover that there are many points of view, and the narrowly focused subject you discussed did, in fact, raise many questions or ideas in your listeners' minds. But in some cases their participation must be drawn out.

A second approach is to pose a situation, and then ask how your audience would hande it. For example, you pose a hypothetical problem and ask members of the audience to suggest how the problem could be solved. Or you rephrase your major points in terms of a problem they are likely to face, and then you invite opposing points of view. Perhaps the solutions you suggested are not the only answers. Other ideas might come up.

By turning what was intended as a relatively passive question-and-answer session into a workshop, you can add more value to your speech. Audience members may respond very enthusiastically to this approach when they would not ask direct questions.

Speakers must assume an active leadership role with their audiences. With this knowledge in hand, you will soon realize that there's little cause for the common nervous condition that all speakers face, and you will be able to conquer your natural fears. You are in a leadership role as speaker. But when you ask members of the audience for questions, they might simply be too passive to respond as you expect. You must then lead them into a different form of participation by challenging them to think. Pose a problem and, instead of giving them the answer, demand one from them. Unless the audience is completely uninterested, you will get some response.

MIXING INTERACTION

Most speaking situations follow the same pattern. A speech is delivered to a very passive audience, and a question-and-answer session follows. But that is not always the best format.

Keeping in mind that audiences are generally passive, there are circumstances where you will do better to invite participation *during* your speech. This is especially true in smaller rooms, with smaller groups, and when your topic is delivered to a peer group. In smaller rooms people are more likely to speak out, whereas they often are intimidated in larger settings. And audiences in large halls feel less comfortable commenting during any phase of your speech.

Example: You outline your speech in four major segments. As you come to the end of each segment, invite audience questions or comments. However, make it clear at this point that you will limit their participation in the interest of time. Say, "Let's take a few minutes for responses. Does anyone have a question, observation, or idea?" When the allotted time has passed, say, "We'll have to move on." Then make a transition into the next segment of your talk.

The interactive format is more interesting for the audience, because people can experience their own participation during the speech. One of the flaws in the speech that is followed by questions and answers is the segregation of the audience's role. When the people in the audience have to wait until the end of your speech, they are forced to remain passive and then to become very active and participate in a limited amount of time, and in a very restricted, formalized manner.

Interaction creates a dialogue and allows you to speak not only in a generally conversational tone, but with individual members of the audience—during your speech. Some of the most instructive and useful speeches take place in this format, even when the audience is fairly large. It helps if your listeners are strongly opinionated and willing to share their thoughts. But if the group is a very passive one, afraid to speak out and share, then the participative format is very difficult to create.

Be flexible. Even if you intend to give your full speech and deal with questions only at the end, you might find it beneficial to change your mind on the spot. If the opportunity presents itself, you could find yourself in a good position to lead the discussion, rather than merely presenting ideas to a passive group.

Example: A speaker makes an important point and gets an immediate reaction. Some members of the audience voice agreement, while others strongly disagree. Instead of going forward as planned, the speaker says, "Obviously, we have some strong opinions. Does anyone want to comment?" Rather than ignoring the importance of a strong audience opinion, the speaker made a wise decision—allowing members of the audience to make their comments at the point where the issue was raised.

It's unusual for audiences to verbally respond to a speaker during the speech itself, except in cases of the most controversial nature. And for you as a speaker, that presents an opportunity that won't often repeat itself. Be willing to let your format vary when the audience is vocal, either in agreement with you or in opposition. One of the most rewarding positions you can be in is to moderate over an audience that is split in its opinions.

The most crucial point to keep in mind, though, is that *you* must always be in control. Don't allow your speech to deteriorate into an audience debate. Once you lose your control, you will not be able to get it back.

Use moderating skills with these guidelines:

1. *Allow only one person to speak at a time.* As soon as a second person interrupts, step in and assert your control.

2. *Once both sides have made their point, get back to your speech.* As long as two sides have points to make, the discussion could go on all day. Use common sense to judge when to stop the interaction. But also keep your ears and eyes open. If more opportunities arise to invite participation, take advantage of them.

3. *Be willing to abandon the format you planned if an interactive discussion is more important than what you were going to say.* This might be a difficult

opportunity to recognize, since it requires you to put aside your outline and admit that something more interesting has developed on its own. But look for the chance. An excellent speaker will see it and know its value.

One speaker discovered the benefits of allowing the hour to take its own course, without expecting it to happen. He intended to cover a range of topics, but when he raised the first one, someone in the audience raised her hand and asked a question. The speaker's answer created another question and comment, and the audience became very involved. The speaker maintained control, offering comments and observations on what was only a small segment of what he had planned to cover. But the audience did most of the work. The speaker realized that there was such a strong level of opinion among the audience on this one issue, that to end the discussion and go on to new topics would be a missed opportunity. He moderated the discussion while maintaining control.

After his speech was over, several members of the audience complimented him for "the best speech they'd ever heard." He quietly pocketed his notes and thanked them.

WORK PROJECT

1. Name three questions that are always on the mind of the audience, and explain why these questions must be addressed in every speech you give.

2. What's the best way to handle a question when you don't know the answer, or when you can't answer briefly?

3. List three points to keep in mind about question-and-answer sessions, and explain why these points are important to you as a speaker.

Epilogue
Speaking and Your Career

Visibility. That's the primary benefit of giving a speech. If you work within an organization, you compete with other people, each with their own career goals. Competition can occur in a positive environment and does not necessarily denote harmful actions. Speaking is one good example of a positive competitive activity.

You will improve your influence within the organization by being willing to take a calculated risk. Grab every opportunity to speak, applying the guidelines and techniques for well-prepared presentations. That means being willing to speak out at staff meetings, symposia, seminars, and conventions your company sponsors, and making yourself available for programs put together by management associations operating locally or nationally.

Visibility presents many opportunities, but also means you must take a risk. The risk factor is always related to the questions every speaker must answer:

- What if I'm so nervous I can't finish?
- What if they ask me something I don't know?
- What could I possibly have to say?
- Why would anyone consider me an expert?

These fears are overcome with self-confidence and with the knowledge of the basic principles for successful speaking. As long as you understand the people in your audience, any topic can be expressed in a context that intrigues and interests them. This applies in all situations except the most extreme mismatches, whether the audience consists of a small gathering of managers in a conference room or in a hall that seats 800 people.

Example: A manager presents a proposal at an executive meeting, with the purpose of requesting that the company invest $20,000 in new furniture and equipment, approve staff increases, and allow the department to double its floor space. There are two ways to approach this task:

1. *The problem approach.* Most requests made in corporate meetings are presented as problems. The idea is introduced, and someone in a position of authority is asked to solve it. This method does *not* get results.

Trying to delegate a problem upward is a poor approach. From the audience's point of view, this is likely to make *you* the problem.

Think about the attendees at the meeting—the people who make decisions in your company. They are your audience, and the issue they confront constantly is running the organization to improve and maintain profits. So when a manager asks for more money, that does not address the audience's interests.

2. *The solution approach.* Keeping the audience in mind, you must ask yourself, "How can I present my ideas so that I will achieve my goals and at the same time gain support from management?"

The answer is not a complicated one: The decision maker is concerned with profits. So the issue must be presented in a way that demonstrates how its approval will improve profits. You must discuss tangible points: the length of time required to recapture the investment, how the bottom line will be directly enhanced, and future savings in operating expenses. Demonstrate your awareness of the problems and pressures your listeners face: that their performance is judged by the profits or losses their decisions create. That's putting your ideas in a context with the audience in mind.

Within your company your ability to communicate has a direct bearing on your career. You will have many opportunities to speak—to one other person, to small groups, and, perhaps, to a more formal audience. In each case the visibility factor works for you as long as you communicate *with* the people in your audience—not from your point of view exclusively, but with their priorities in mind. If you do that, the circle of enthusiasm will work for you. That's the kind of visibility you need in order to advance in the organization.

Managers in the middle levels might convince themselves that to be effective speakers they need the clout of position. The assumption is that a vice president or other corporate officer is obviously qualified to speak on any topic and naturally possesses self-confidence. The truth is that if you don't develop self-confidence now, you won't automatically acquire it as you gain a bigger title.

Rank has nothing to do with the ability to speak confidently and effectively. Enthusiasm works for everyone who follows the basic guidelines. Once you stand up and begin to speak, the people in the audience don't care about your title, nor are they concerned with your experience or education. Their reaction will be based on how well you communicate, and on whether or not you speak to their concerns. As long as you make that connection, you ensure success as a speaker.

Appendix
Work Project Answers

CHAPTER 1

1. The four possible negative responses are criticism, dislike, hostility, and apathy.

    Criticism should be welcomed, for only through construction advice can you improve. Don't view criticism as a negative reaction, but as one that can help you to become a more accomplished speaker.

    There's not much you can do if your audience dislikes you; however, you should recognize this as an individual and not a group response in most cases. The best way to deal with it is to depend on your own self-confidence, and put it aside.

    A hostile response is unlikely from the audience as a whole. If it does occur, it's probably a sign that you did not prepare with your audience in mind. And an individual's hostility cannot be helped; don't let that response inhibit your future speaking ability.

    Apathy is the most difficult response of all. Because it is the *absence* of feedback, you are given no indication beyond the sense that something is wrong. The fact is, apathy is usually the speaker's own fault. You can best deal with it by honestly evaluating your speaking techniques, discovering what's lacking, and correcting the problem.
2. Seven distinct exercises should be practiced to help you control and direct your nerves:
    a. Concentrate on an object to channel energy.
    b. Stop fighting your nerves and accept the condition as a human response to being on the spot.

    c. Tense and relax your muscles, to help take away the feeling of being out of control.

    d. Stretch your muscles to relax.

    e. Speak with someone else to get your mind away from the fear of appearing nervous.

    f. Go through your personal self-esteem checklist to put yourself in the best frame of mind.

    g. Increase your energy level just before you begin to speak so that your nervousness will be directed toward delivering an energetic speech.

3. First, find and use an individual audience ally. Deliver your speech directly to that person, who preferably will be seated at the back of the room. Second, attempt to meet members of your audience before you speak, even if it's just to shake hands and introduce yourself. And third, if all else fails, begin your speech by admitting your nervousness; that simple act will probably make the fear disappear at once.

CHAPTER 2

1 Plan to script your opening and closing statements, and the key points in the body of your speech. When you deliver your speech, your style should be as conversational as possible. You add contrast and emphasis, however, by pausing to read a key point from a card or page.

2. Your three best sources are your own observations and ideas, your experiences, and your knowledge. A useful and informative speech is invariably rooted in these three sources. Putting too much effort into quoting statistics and other sources to prove the point you're trying to make only masks your personality. And audiences will react more to you and the way you present yourself than to the content of your speech.

3. To round out your outline, consider speaking with other managers, employees, and executives in your company. Each of these groups has a point of view about your subject different than your own point of view. If your audience consists of members of these groups, you

will be better able to identify with their cares and concerns if you
first understand their point of view.

CHAPTER 3

1. There are many self-defeating mental attitudes that speakers adopt
    out of fear. This is a natural condition and response. Among the
    most common are:
    a. What could I say that others would find interesting?
    b. I don't have enough to say to fill up an entire hour.
    c. Someone else could do a better job.
    All three of these attitudes can be overcome once you acknowledge
    your own expertise. To address each of the sample points:
    a. Just because your area of knowledge is limited does not mean it
        cannot be interesting. By focusing your speech and identifying
        with your audience, it's up to you to make your subject an
        interesting, provocative one.
    b. Don't waste your energy worrying about how to fill up a time
        slot. Concentrate on the mental preparation of your speech, and
        organize a brief but well-focused outline. The problem will take
        care of itself if you tailor your speech to the audience.
    c. No one else can do a better job of discussing your area of
        expertise, no matter how much experience he or she has as a
        speaker. All of us, even those who have spoken in public many
        times, are nervous each time we get up to speak. You can do just
        as well if you maintain *your* focus, in the interest of developing a
        focus for your audience.
2. Putting an outline on one or more sheets of paper is appropriate only
    if you'll be able to put the paper down on a podium. You will not
    want to hold your outline in your hand, because that inhibits your
    ability to communicate with the people in your audience. It acts as a
    wall between you and them. And if you are nervous, the shaking of
    your hands will seem worse when the paper shakes as well. Index
    cards give you freedom of movement and gesture. And a legal pad
    will not shake even when your hands are out of control.

3. Many people believe they have a greater degree of control with smaller groups and the most control in a one-to-one meeting. In fact, control passes back and forth in one-to-one situations and varies with moderately sized groups. The larger the audience, the greater the degree of control you have as a speaker. A large audience is a single, passive entity. Thus, in an analysis of the fear of speaking, a very large group is the least threatening, and smaller groups will present greater problems for you as a speaker.

CHAPTER 4

1. The primary form of expertise required of any speaker is a comprehension of who the people in the audience are and what they need and want to hear. Successful speakers understand their audiences well. While you must be sure to limit your speaking topics to areas of interest to you, the key is always the people in the audience. Your message must be expressed in the context of *their* interests.

   Each time you give a speech, your message must be specifically focused, not only in terms of what you will discuss, but also in terms of who you are addressing. Whenever you prepare a speech, be sure to find out who will attend. If you know nothing about the concerns of the people in your audience, ask questions and get different points of view. Then structure your speech to address your topic with their concerns in mind.

2. Marketing and accounting managers often find themselves polarized by a completely different set of priorities. This problem of unlike interests affects all of us to a degree. The task for a marketing manager who is asked to speak before accountants is to identify that audience's concerns, problems, and interests—as they apply to a topic.

   Possible ideas for speech subjects could include:

   "Ideas for Improving Information Flow Between Departments"
   "Income Forecasting: A Point of View From the Field"
   "Record Keeping: Where Salespeople Need Your Help"

3. As you attempt to draw up a list of topics on which you will be comfortable speaking, don't limit yourself to immediate areas in which you are involved on a day-to-day basis. And don't be concerned at first with whether or not an audience will find your topic interesting. Simply examine your background and experience. You will discover that you are an expert on a wide range of ideas.

   Example: The manager of a customer service department could speak to the people in any audience on the importance of the role *they* play in developing customer loyalty; how the customer service department can be used as a resource center; and how the department serves not only the customer, but other departments as well.

   Example: A manager of the records department could address a group of other managers on how to organize their own file retrieval system; the alternatives in record storage; and how efficient storage systems save time and money.

   In any situation address your listeners with *their* interests in mind. Some helpful generalizations follow:
   a. Corporate executives: At this level, members of the audience are responsible for controlling costs and creating profits, and for delegating responsibility to others. That gives you the focus of any message for a group of executives.
   b. A peer group: This level has a good deal in common with you, so the best approach is to identify common problems and then suggest possible solutions. In a peer group setting, plan to invite interaction. Chances are that a lively discussion will enrich your presentation and result in valuable information for everyone present.
   c. College students: The emphasis here must be on a topic of interest to audience members very different from those you are used to dealing with. They might be concerned with selecting a career, identifying the realities of the business world, or understanding the workings of the corporate culture.

CHAPTER 5

1. Five attributes were explained in this chapter. They are:
   a. Simplicity: No subject is so complex that it cannot be expressed in direct, simple terms. In fact, the more complex a subject is

thought to be, the more the audience will appreciate a clear discussion.

b. Brevity: The longer your speech, the less interest you can expect from the audience. Stay within your allotted time, express yourself and communicate your message as briefly as possible, and refuse to accept the notion that long speeches are better than short ones.

c. Focus: Keep your topic as narrow as possible. If you attempt to present too broad a range of subjects, the result will be a rambling and confusing presentation.

d. Awareness: Don't forget the people in your audience. They must remain interested in order for your speech to succeed. Thus, you must tailor your message so that it speaks directly to them.

e. Energy: Audiences cannot help but respond to an energetic, enthusiastic speaker. Bring your personal energy and sincerity to the podium, and convey it to your audience.

2. Speakers must face the dilemma of deciding how to open their speech. The introduction is the most difficult and most dangerous segment, because you must take charge and get the audience's attention and appreciation as quickly as possible. Some methods for accomplishing this are:

a. Humor: Starting with a joke or anecdote will immediately do away with nervousness, as long as the humorous opening goes over. The humorous opening is the easiest way to start out, but it should lead naturally to the more important statement you really want to make. Be aware of the danger in overusing jokes or trying the same material too often or on dissimilar audiences.

b. Statistics: Use statistics that have a lot to do with your topic and that speak directly to the audience. The more alarming or sensational the statistic, the better—as long as it's appropriate. Don't depend so heavily on a shocking statistic that the statement you make afterward is relatively tame. You must be prepared to follow the statistic with a high-energy statement that holds the audience's interest.

c. Questions: When you begin by asking the people in your audience a question—accompanied by the request for a show of hands—they are immediately involved. However, be careful in the phrasing of the question. Don't insult or patronize the audience.

3. Following a strong introduction, some speakers forget the importance of holding the audience's attention. This is a constant effort. Some ideas:

   a. Stay with the theme: Don't allow yourself to wander from a narrowly focused topic. If you do wander, the audience's attention will wander, too—in a different direction.

   b. Change the pace: Audiences expect to be kept interested, and a continuously low or high level of energy will put them to sleep. Use pauses, changes in tone of voice, volume, and speed of speaking to alter the pace.

   c. Keep it flowing smoothly: Use transitions to move from one point to another. If you do not, the audience will not be able to follow your train of thought.

   d. Include the people in your audience: Ask for participation through raising of hands, or lead them through an exercise requiring them to write something down. Don't make your speech in isolation, but take every opportunity to make the audience feel involved.

   e. Make it personal: Illustrate key points with examples from your own experiences. Tell the members of your audience what you have to say in a manner they can relate to, and you will hold their interest throughout your speech.

CHAPTER 6

1. Prepare as far as possible in advance so that you can tailor your speech to the environment and audience size that is being planned. Your questions should include the estimated audience size, whether or not you will speak from a stage, the planned seating arrangement, whether you will have a podium or a microphone, the separation (if any) between you and the audience, and your placement on the agenda.

   Also be prepared for last-minute changes. For example, agendas often are not finalized until the last week or two before a seminar, and your slot might be changed because another speaker's schedule does not fit with the plan. So in addition to planning ahead, you must be flexible enough to accept changes.

2. When you find that the environment is different than what you planned for, be ready to alter the method of delivery. In this case turning statements into questions will draw the audience into the speech:
    a. How many of you have experienced the frustration of trying to get results in a bureaucratic system?
    b. Any ideas on how to get results, even when management moves slowly?
    c. Does anyone have a thought on how to deal with someone who's resisting change?
3. Separation from your audience, represented by physical distance, a podium, and the large, passive audience mentality, can be used as shields. However, you can improve communication skills by stepping away from the podium at key points in your speech; using pauses effectively to get the audience's attention; varying your voice's tempo and volume; and leaving the podium to get closer to your audience during the question-and-answer phase.

CHAPTER 7

1. Audiences are on your side. They want you to do well as a speaker, for three reasons:
    a. The people in the audience have good reasons for attending the meeting. In some situations they have paid to attend and want valuable information. In other situations they are there to learn as part of their job.
    b. Audience members are sympathetic to you as a speaker. Either they have spoken before and know how difficult it is to stand up in front of others, or they have never spoken and have great respect for those who are able to give a good speech.
    c. For most people, watching a nervous speaker is a painful experience. Few of us want to see someone else having difficulty and would prefer seeing others succeed.
2. Whenever you perceive one audience and find yourself in front of another, you must be prepared to identify with the group—regardless of topic. For example, in discussing report preparation, executives

will gain insights if you share with them the techniques they can use to better communicate with subordinates when giving out assignments. Many reports are not well directed because assignments are vague. As a topic for a speech, this will provide value to the audience.

3. Judge your audience by:

   a. Attendance: The size of the audience should determine the style to use in delivering your speech.

   b. Age: The average age of people in your audience will often determine whether or not they can identify with your message. Your point of view must be sensitive to different age groups.

   c. Sex: Think about the tone and emphasis of your message if the audience is all-male or all-female. This is especially important when the audience is of the opposite sex.

   d. Education: Based on occupation or on information supplied to you by the meeting organizer, your topic should be approached with licensing and formal educations in mind.

   e. Rank: Corporate rank of the people in your audience is essential to their response. Most business topics can be tailored or modified to suit any rank.

   f. Economics: Be aware of the financial status of your audience as you prepare your outline.

   g. Motives: You must know why the people in the audience are there and how that effects what they expect to learn from you.

   h. Attitudes: Do the people in your audience have any noteworthy attitudes about the topic, their own occupation, or your occupation? These must be considered if you intend to gain the audience's respect and attention.

   i. Agenda: The time and place on the agenda will make a difference in how the audience receives your message.

CHAPTER 8

1. The paragraph contains poor rhythm, as each sentence is about the same length. This choppy style can easily be given more variety. For example:

Budget development is a time-consuming process. If you deal with it quickly or halfway, you will suffer the consequences. You'll have to live with it for the entire year.

2. Always look for places where unnecessary words can be removed, or where ideas can be expressed simply. For example:
   a. I think . . .
   b. Managers . . .
   c. Our people count . . .
   d. Planning works . . .

3. A strong, specific phrase is better received by audiences. Awkward or qualified statements tend to go over people's heads, and when they find their way into your speech the audience will not pay attention or absorb your ideas. The statements should be rewritten:
   a. We are responsible.
   b. The manager's job is timely completion.
   c. You cannot solve every problem.

CHAPTER 9

1. Always anticipate the worst when working with visual aids, especially if plugged-in equipment is essential to their use. Some examples of problems you might not anticipate without a rehearsal:

   - The audience cannot see the screen from all sides of the room.
   - Lettering is not large enough for everyone to read.
   - The equipment doesn't work.
   - No screen is supplied.
   - There is too much light.
   - No one is available to dim the lights or close the drapes.
   - Your assistant doesn't know how to use the machine.
   - Slides or overheads are out of order.
   - Your assistant doesn't know when to go to the next slide or overhead.

To avoid these problems, run through the portion of your speech that requires assistance, and look for the problems you have not anticipated.

2. There are at least four important criteria for deciding whether or not to use visuals:
   a. Complexity of the material: If you must discuss information that is too complex to explain verbally, visual aids can help to simplify your message.
   b. Audience use: Visual aids are the most valuable when the audience will use the material in some way. For example, an explanation of procedures given during a training seminar is helped with the use of flow charts and forms. These should be accompanied by actual samples included in an audience kit.
   c. Retention: Visual aids help the audience retain important information. You can use visual aids to emphasize key points or to express your main ideas—a technique used in sales seminars that can also be applied in other situations.
   d. Need: Whenever the audience needs the help of a visual aid, or when you as a speaker can better explain your message when it is seen as well, plan a limited but effective use of slides or overheads.
3. The points to keep in mind are:
   a. You are the leader: Your speech is always better when the focus of attention is on you, not on the visual aid.
   b. Direction of the message: Always speak to your audience and never to the visual.
   c. Focus: Concentrate on your main message, and never allow a visual aid to act as a substitute for what you have to say.
   d. Simplicity: Visuals that are overly complex add nothing to your speech, may confuse the audience, and distract from you.
   e. Rehearse: Eliminate any potential problems by running through the portion of your speech involving visual aids.
   f. Position: Decide where to stand so that you do not block the audience's view of your visual, and so that you are not blocked from view by the visual.
   g. Limit use: Show the visual only when it applies to what you are discussing at that moment. Never show a visual ahead of time; and when you're through, remove it from the audience's view.

CHAPTER 10

1. The moderator's job is to maintain control over the presentation, which includes enforcing the time limit rules. In order to

keep speakers to these limits, you must be able to assert control. Consider the use of a card advising the speaker that time is up, or place a stopwatch on the panelists' table. If the speaker does not respond, you will have to interrupt as politely as possible and allow the program to continue.

2. Business meetings are highly interactive and you should not prepare for them in the same way you would for a speech. When you're addressing a large group, the audience is very passive. However, a business meeting is set up to serve as a dialogue. Be prepared to present your main points briefly and up front, and then to let the meeting run its own course. If you are in charge, you will have to cut off discussion to cover all agenda items. If someone else is in charge, all you can do is participate, present your material, and respond to questions and comments.

CHAPTER 11

1. Every audience asks you, as a speaker, to answer these unspoken questions during your speech:
   a. Who are you and what do you have to say? You must begin each speech by addressing this issue, and if you can answer in a way that is intriguing and interesting to the audience, you're off to a good start.
   b. How will I benefit from listening to you? The people in every audience expect to receive something of value from you as a result of hearing your speech. If you cannot deliver, then you have no purpose in speaking. But if you always approach your outline with this point in mind, you will never fail to give them something that benefits them.
   c. Are you going to talk to me directly? There is a vast difference between a lecture and a dialogue. Strive for honest dialogue with your audience. Never assume the posture of an instructor whose purpose is to teach the audience something, especially how to think. Always think of your task as an exercise in teamwork, even when the audience is passive.
   d. Will you make it interesting? As long as you want to interest your audience, and as long as you put your energy and enthusiasm into

the task, you will not fail in your attempt to answer this question affirmatively. Audiences fear the uninteresting speaker, because time goes very slowly when the speaker fails to inspire.

e. Are you going to end on time? Audiences will always be grateful when speakers respect the agenda, especially if you address them just before lunch or at the last hour of the day.

2. The best of speeches can be made monotonous by poor handling of the question–and–answer session. Two critical rules to remember are:

a. When you do not know the answer, admit that you do not know. Then follow up by promising to find the answer and to give it to the person as soon as possible.

b. If you cannot answer a question in two minutes or less, ask the questioner to meet with you after your session is completed so that other people can have the chance to ask their questions.

3. Remember these important points about the question-and-answer session:

a. Keep your energy level up. Your speech is not over until you leave the podium.

b. Be aware of the message you convey. Pay attention to your own body language, maintain eye contact, and don't become overly relaxed.

c. Listen carefully to the full question. Don't interrupt unless the question itself becomes a speech.

d. Keep your answers simple. The briefer your answer, the better.

e. Turn negatives into positives. Don't allow the tone of an optimistic speech to deteriorate into a downbeat mood.

f. Respect the questioner. Don't ridicule or insult anyone. Deal with hostility directly and professionally, and then move on to the next question.

Index